Explaining the Faith Series

UNDERSTANDING THE SACRAMENTS

God's Grace Guaranteed!

by Fr. Chris Alar, MIC

MARIAN PRESS
STOCKBRIDGE MA 01263

©2025 Marian Fathers of the Immaculate Conception of the B.V.M.
All rights reserved.

Available from:
Marian Helpers Center
Stockbridge, MA 01263
Prayerline: 1-800-804-3823
Orderline: 1-800-462-7426

Websites:
ShopMercy.org
Marian.org
TheDivineMercy.org
DivineMercyPlus.org

Library of Congress Catalog Number: 2025935333
ISBN: 978-1-59614-645-7

Cover and layout by Kathy Szpak

Imprimi Potest:
Most Rev. Joseph Roesch, MIC
Superior General
Congregation of Marian Fathers of the Immaculate Conception of the B.V.M.
Solemnity of the Annunciation of the Lord
March 25, 2025

Nihil Obstat:
Robert A. Stackpole, STD
Censor Deputatus
March 25, 2025

Excerpts from the English translation of the *Catechism of the Catholic Church* for use in the United States of America Copyright © 1994, United States Catholic Conference, Inc. — Libreria Editrice Vaticana. English translation of the *Catechism of the Catholic Church:* Modifications from the Editio Typica copyright © 1997, United States Conference of Catholic Bishops — Libreria Editrice Vaticana.

Scripture quotations are from two sources: the New Revised Standard Version Bible (Catholic Edition, copyright © 1989, 1993 National Council of the Churches of Christ in the United States of America. All rights reserved. nrsbibles.org) and, where noted, from the New American Bible (revised edition © 2010, 1991, 1986, 1970 Confraternity of Christian Doctrine, Washington, D.C. All rights reserved).

Texts contained in this work derived whole or in part from liturgical texts are copyrighted by the International Commission on English in the Liturgy (ICEL).

Contents

INTRODUCTION 1
Guaranteed Grace 4
What is a Sacrament? 8
The Quickest, Easiest, Surest Way 11
Your Soul is Marked Forever 12

THE SACRAMENTS OF INITIATION 15
Baptism 17
Form, Matter, Minister 18
Effects of Baptism 22
Indelible Mark 23
(Infant) Baptism in Scripture and Tradition 25

Confirmation 33
Gifts and Fruits of the Holy Spirit 34
Form, Matter, Minister 38
Confirmation in the Bible 40
Confirmation Age 43

Holy Eucharist 45
Form, Matter, Minister 46
What is the Eucharistic Sacrifice? 48
The Eucharist in Scripture 51
Who May Receive? 52
It's Not Just a Symbol 53
Eucharistic Miracles 57
The Meaning of the Mass 61

THE SACRAMENTS OF HEALING 65
Reconciliation (Penance or Confession) 67
Form, Matter, Minister 69
What is Sin? 70
How to Prepare for a Good Confession 72
How to Make a Good Confession 79
Where is Confession in the Bible? 81
Confess to a Man? *In Persona Christi* 83
Doctor of the Soul 86
Is Your Confession Valid? 88
Sin and Temporal Punishment 90

Are All Sins Forgivable? 94
Summary of Why We Need Confession 96

Anointing of the Sick 99
Form, Matter, Minister 100
Anointing of the Sick in Scripture 101
When to Receive This Sacrament 103
Last Rites? 104

THE SACRAMENTS OF SERVICE 109
Holy Orders 111
Form, Matter, Minister 113
The Priesthood in Scripture 115
Call No Man "Father"? 119
What About Married Priests or Women Priests? 120
Surprisingly, It is Great Joy! 123
The Scandal 124
Pray for Priests 127

Matrimony 131
Form, Matter, Minister 134
Three Objectives of Marriage 137
Women Do *What*? 139
Divorce 142
Is Your Marriage Valid? Annulments 146
Some Interesting Final Points 149

AFTERWORD: Outside the Church,
There is No Salvation 151
In the Bible, Who Can Be Saved? 155
Ignorance and Knowledge 156
What About Non-Catholics and Non-Christians? 158
How to Get to Heaven 161

About the Author 165
Endnotes 167

~ INTRODUCTION ~

I often get asked, as you may too, "What makes the Catholic Church different from any other Christian church?" While the answer is simple, it comes in two parts. First, the Catholic Church is the only church founded by Jesus Christ Himself. All the Protestant Christian churches were founded by an ordinary man or woman. Name any other Christian denomination and we can tell you who founded it. Baptist? Founded by John Smyth in 1609. Anglican? Founded by King Henry VIII in 1534. Methodist? Founded by John Wesley in the mid-18th century. We can continue this 45,000 more times if needed, because that is the estimated number of Christian denominations in the world today. But recall our Lord's words in Matthew 16:18: "I tell you, you are Peter, and on this rock I will build my church, and the gates of Hades [hell] will not prevail against it." So which Church was Christ referring to? Answer: *The Catholic Church.*

If you are reading this, you may be thinking to yourself, *That's fine, Fr. Chris, but maybe the Catholic Church today has nothing to do whatsoever with the Church established by Jesus Christ. How do we know the Catholic Church really isn't man-made?* While that is a fair question, we can come to the answer through some logical thought. The Catholic Church isn't man-made but "God-made," as Jesus passed His authority from His apostles to His Church. That is why Sacred Apostolic Tradition, not man-made tradition, is in the Bible, and why St. Paul said to hold fast to the traditions that he taught, both oral and written (see 2 Thess 2:15). So, when you hear someone say, "I don't follow the teachings of men," you may say, "Neither do I. In fact, I follow the teachings of God explained by the very men Christ entrusted to teach us." Christ gave His authority to the apostles and then gave them authority to pass it down (see Mt 28:20; the Acts of the Apostles, especially Acts 14:23; 1 Tim 1:3; and Tit 1:5). As St. Paul said, "What you hear from me entrust to faithful men, who will be able to teach others also" (2 Tim 2:2). *Sola Scriptura*, which means "Bible only," is not in the Bible, but Apostolic Tradition is, and that gives the Church part of her authority (along with Scripture and the Magisterium). In 1 Timothy 3:15, Paul called the Church "the pillar and foundation of the truth" because Christ established the chair of the papacy and placed Peter upon it (see Mt 16:18). In Colossians 1:18, Paul also said Jesus is the head of the body, which is the Church. So, contrary to common belief, the Church isn't man-made, but rather God-made, as we said.

Let's return to the words directly from Jesus: "You are Peter and upon this rock **I** will build **my** Church" (Mt 16:18; my emphasis). He did not say, "**You** will build **your** Church." Jesus founded His Church at Pentecost (Acts 2:14) after having earlier breathed the Holy Spirit upon the apostles. Why would we not believe that the Holy Spirit has remained upon this Church until the present day? It makes sense, because this would be true to Jesus' promise to Peter that the "gates of hell will not prevail against it" (Mt 16:18). At the birth of the Church at Pentecost, Peter stood up to lead the apostles as Jesus commanded him (Acts 1:15). Thus, Jesus founded His Church upon *people*, not principles. Jesus did not say, "You are the Bible and upon this book I will build my Church," since there was no Bible in the room that day. Remember, the Church was born 350 years before the Church pieced together the New Testament Bible out of hundreds of letters and other books that became the canon of Scripture, the same 27 books all Christians, even non-Catholics, use today. Since the Mass predates the Bible, it is logical to believe most Church scholars who state that the Bible was actually compiled from those many writings to be read at the Mass! This is why the Catholic faith has the same three-legged faith "stool" as the Jews had: Scripture, Sacred Tradition, and a Magisterium. All are of God.

But again, which Church are we talking about? Well, in addition to Christ establishing the papacy mentioned above, for more than 1,500 years there was no other Christian ("Petrine") church other than the Catholic Church. Only the Catholic Church can claim Apostolic Succession, meaning that from St. Peter to the present day there is an unbroken line of succession of popes, bishops, and priests, each one laying on hands, conferring the Sacrament of Holy Orders to the next man to serve Christ and His Church on earth. Thus, every single Catholic clergyman alive today can physically be traced in a direct line (by laying on of hands) back to one of the apostles, and thus to Christ Himself. It is daunting to realize that Christ touched one of the apostle's heads to bestow the Holy Spirit, who then touched someone else's head, who then touched another, all the way directly to me. Only a Catholic priest can claim to be part of this succession. (Yes, the Orthodox Church can also make this claim, so more on that in a moment.) There can only be one Truth, and since all religions teach something different or they wouldn't be different religions, what religion teaches the fullness of the Truth? The most logical answer would be the one that Jesus Christ Himself started, the Roman Catholic Church (as we will show).

The second aspect that distinguishes the Catholic Church from any other church is the subject of this book: the Sacraments. Recall that there are seven: Baptism, Confirmation, Holy Eucharist, Reconciliation (Penance or Confession), Anointing of the Sick, Holy Orders (Ordination), and Matrimony. The Sacraments are so important that I had a class for each of the seven in seminary. I have always said that my time in seminary was the best time of my life, and if I could go back in time, back to seminary would be my choice.

Well, now I have pulled out all of my meticulous notes, along with the help of our theologian Chris Sparks, and I am going to share them with you, so that you may go back to seminary with me, but without having to go to class, take tests, or pay tuition! In this book, join me to learn what I learned at seminary and learn what all Catholics should have learned in their faith formation process. Remember, as St. Thomas Aquinas taught (quoting St. Augustine before him), "You cannot love what you do not know."[1]

Thus, I believe that if you come to know what is in this book, given in a summary-type format, you will come to love your Catholic faith more deeply, in a way that will change your life! If you have already learned about the Sacraments, then I believe this book can still be a good review for you and perhaps even a source of some new information.

One point of clarification before I proceed. The churches of the Eastern Orthodox communion separated from the Roman Catholic Church in 1054 ("The Great Schism"). But since they descend from the Petrine Church, they validly claim authentic Apostolic Succession, and therefore validly-ordained priests. In fact, they also have all seven Sacraments. The Sacraments they possess today are the same that they took with them when they fell out of communion with Rome almost 1,000 years ago. So, can Roman Catholics receive Sacraments in an Eastern Orthodox church? Yes, but only in an emergency or an extraordinary situation — for instance, if a person is dying and a Roman Catholic priest is not available, or if there is no access to a Roman Catholic church to fulfill one's Sunday obligation. When I write in this book about the Sacraments and their uniqueness, I am speaking on behalf of the Roman Catholic Church, but always with respect for our Orthodox brethren and their valid Sacraments. Now, let's look at a few things first.

Guaranteed Grace

The reason the Sacraments are so important is that the Holy Spirit acts through them. They are not just symbols of grace — they are actual grace itself! The Sacraments give us guaranteed grace and eternal life if we cooperate with this grace. You can't get anything more important. The Holy Spirit gives us the Church, and the Church in return gives us the Sacraments. Saint John Henry Newman declared, "The visible world still remains without its divine interpretation; Holy Church in her sacraments and her hierarchical appointments will remain, even to the end of the world."[2] The Sacraments are connected to ultimately form you into a disciple of Christ. Your spiritual life begins at Baptism. It is matured at Confirmation. Your soul is renewed in Reconciliation after you fall into sin. Your spirit and, perhaps, your body are healed with the Anointing of the Sick. Families are made with Marriage. The Church is sustained through Holy Orders by giving us priests to give us the Sacraments. And your soul is fed and sustained throughout this whole process because Christ is present in the Eucharist that you receive at Holy Communion.

The Sacraments are what Christ did on Earth for our salvation. God commanded us to receive the Sacraments as all seven are in the Bible:

> **Baptism:** Jesus is baptized by John and hears the Great Commission: "Jesus came from Nazareth of Galilee and was baptized by John in the Jordan. And just as he was coming up out of the water, he saw the heavens torn apart and the Spirit descending like a dove on him. And a voice came from heaven, 'You are my Son, the Beloved; with you I am well pleased'" (Mk 1:9-11).[3] "Go, therefore, and make disciples of all nations, baptizing them in the name of the Father, and of the Son, and of the holy Spirit" (Mt 28:19).
>
> **Eucharist:** Jesus said, "I am the living bread that came down from heaven. Whoever eats of this bread will live forever; and the bread that I will

give for the life of the world is my flesh. ... Very truly, I say to you, unless you eat the flesh of the Son of Man and drink his blood, you have no life in you. Those who eat my flesh and drink my blood have eternal life, and I will raise them up on the last day" (Jn 6:51, 53-54).

Confession: Jesus said, "Whatever you bind on earth shall be bound in heaven, and whatever you loose on earth will be loosed in Heaven" (Mt 16:19; also Mt 18:18; Jn 20:23).

Anointing of the Sick: The Book of James says to confess your sins to one another after speaking of the presbyters (elders): "Are any among you sick? They should call for the elders of the church and have them pray over them, anointing them with oil in the name of the Lord. The prayer of faith will save the sick, and the Lord will raise them up; and anyone who has committed sins will be forgiven" (Jas 5:14-15).

Priesthood: As for the washing of the feet, which was part of the ordination rite in the Aaronic priesthood, Jesus said, "So if I, your Lord and Teacher, have washed your feet, you also ought to wash one another's feet. For I have set you an example, that you also should do as I have done to you" (Jn 13:14-15). Titus 1:5 mentions that pastors were "ordained" in each city in Crete. Acts 13:2-4 describes the Holy Spirit setting apart Barnabas and Saul for the work to which He has called them. Acts 14:23 mentions Paul and Barnabas directing the appointment or ordination of elders "in each church" in Galatia.

Marriage: In Matthew 19:4-6, Jesus affirms the biblical view of marriage as a union between one man and one woman, citing Genesis 2:24 to support this. The Wedding at Cana, the setting for Jesus' first miracle: "On the third day there was a wedding in Cana of Galilee, and the mother of Jesus was there. Jesus and his disciples had also been invited to the wedding" (Jn 2:1-2). Regarding Ephesians 5:22-33, this passage provides guidance for marriage, emphasizing the roles of husbands and wives, and the importance of submission, love, and respect within marriage.

Confirmation: The Sacrament of Confirmation is found in Bible passages such as Acts 8:14–17, 9:17, 19:6, and Hebrews 6:2, which speak of a laying on of hands for the purpose of bestowing the Holy Spirit. Sealing with the Holy Spirit at Pentecost: "All of them were filled with the Holy Spirit and began to speak in other languages, as the Spirit gave them ability" (Acts 2:4). In Ephesians 4:30, the Holy Spirit is described as a "seal" or "mark" on believers.

The Catholic Church is the only religion that formalized all seven Sacraments, and offers guaranteed grace through them all. Yes, other religions such as the Anglican Church believe in ordination (but have broken Apostolic Succession by ordaining women), for example, but in terms of the guaranteed grace that we receive in Confession or the Eucharist, this is uniquely Catholic. Without the Sacraments, the Catholic Church is just another storefront church, one among the thousands of Christian denominations in the world today.

What is a Sacrament?

As we said, a Sacrament is not just a symbol. It does something! It actually conveys grace to the soul when you receive it. If you're properly disposed (ready to receive it), the grace is guaranteed because the Church, established by Christ and given His authority, promises that. The Bible does, too.

A Sacrament is an "efficacious" sign (meaning it does something) of God's grace, instituted by Christ, entrusted to the Church, by which divine life is instilled in us. Wow! How many Catholics think about this? Here is something that Jesus Himself instituted, and is given to us to instill divine life in us; therefore, Sacraments are not something you want to ignore — or worse, reject. That is why as Catholics they're something we need to receive regularly. The Sacraments are efficacious *ex opere operato* (by the very fact that the sacramental action is performed) because it is Christ who acts in the Sacraments and communicates the grace. Why? In the flesh of Jesus, the spiritual and human physical realms meet (we speak more on *form* and *matter* later), so a Sacrament is something that has both a physical and spiritual reality that brings grace.

A few years ago, I had the grace and privilege of going on a pilgrimage to the Holy Land. While there, I had the honor of visiting what tradition claims to be the Upper Room that we read about in Scripture. I was in awe as I was standing in the area where Jesus purportedly gathered His Twelve Apostles, and the area where four of the seven Sacraments were instituted by Christ in the Bible: the Eucharist, Holy Orders, Confession, and Confirmation.

Because Christ gave us these channels of grace, it is time to explore the Sacraments in thorough detail via this easy-to-read book so that you will come to appreciate even more these greatest of all gifts.

Because of their effects, Sacraments are organized into three categories. First, the **Sacraments of Initiation:**

Baptism, Confirmation, and the Eucharist. The faithful are born anew by Baptism. We are strengthened in Confirmation and nourished by the Eucharist. That is why daily Mass is encouraged. You need earthly food every day to move forward physically, and so does your soul need the spiritual food of the Eucharist.

Next we have the **Sacraments of Healing:** Reconciliation (Penance or Confession) and the Anointing of the Sick. If we go to a doctor to heal our body, why wouldn't we believe we need to go to a doctor for our soul (the priest) in Confession? Anointing of the Sick, as we said, heals the soul and, hopefully, the body as well.

Lastly, the **Sacraments of Service:** Matrimony and Holy Orders. If you are married, your service is to your spouse and your family, and if you are an ordained priest, your service is to your congregation. My service is to educate you in the faith and offer the Sacraments, so you can know God more to love Him more (remember St. Thomas Aquinas) and ultimately get to Heaven.

Tying this all together, St. Thomas Aquinas also said that all of the Sacraments are directed to the Holy Eucharist: "The highest place belongs to the sacraments whereby man is sanctified: chief of which is the sacrament itself of the Eucharist. ... Baptism is the beginning of the spiritual life, and the door of the sacraments; whereas the Eucharist is, as it were, the consummation of the spiritual life, and the end of all the sacraments."[4] Each Sacrament leads us to the heart of life in Christ, the Eucharist: the "source and summit" of our Catholic faith (*Catechism*, 1324). You see, all Sacraments give us grace. But the Holy Eucharist gives us Jesus Himself. That's why it's the greatest ("the highest place") of the seven Sacraments, even greater than Baptism. Baptism removes the effects of original sin, but each time we worthily receive the Eucharist we're implanting Jesus Himself into our body and soul; He comes to strengthen and nourish us spiritually. Think about it!

In one of my Sacraments classes at Holy Apostles Seminary in Cromwell, Connecticut, the teacher, Fr. Brian Mulcahy, a Dominican priest, said something that I'll never forget: "You and I have access to the Trinity in ways far greater than the apostles did. That's because we have the fullness of the Sacraments." To me that's amazing, even beyond comprehension. It means that Christ's Resurrection and Ascension into Heaven allowed the Holy Spirit to come down upon us, opening the floodgates to the wellspring of Divine Mercy. And so, the grace of the Church showers down upon the world the Blood and the Water that brought forth the birth of the Church in the grace given through the Holy Spirit. This is something that the people before Christ — the Patriarchs we read about in the Old Testament like Moses and David — strongly desired. But we have it now, in the Sacraments, which is incredible! Saint John Henry Newman said, "The Spirit came to finish in us, what Christ had finished in Himself, but left unfinished as regards us. ... As a light placed in a room pours out its rays on all sides, so the presence of the Holy Spirit imbues us with life, strength, holiness, love, acceptableness, righteousness."[5] Did you think God was going to leave us without His grace after ascending to the Father? No — He is with us in the Eucharist — Body, Blood, Soul, and Divinity. As my all-time favorite pope, Leo XIII, put it, "That which now takes place in the Church is the most perfect possible, and will last until that day when the Church herself, having passed through her militant career, shall be taken up into the joy of the saints triumphing in heaven."[6]

We know that the Sacraments give us grace to heal, such as the healing power in the confessional, in an anointing of the sick, and the healing grace of the Eucharist, but we forget that the Sacraments also strengthen us for this battle we are in, that of spiritual warfare. "Faith and the sacraments are two complementary aspects of ecclesial life," wrote Pope Benedict XVI. "Awakened by the preaching of God's word, faith is nourished and grows in the grace-filled encounter with the Risen Lord which takes place in the sacraments."[7] Saint Francis de Sales put it this way: "The Sacraments are, so to say, the channels through which God comes down into us, just as through prayer we throw ourselves into God. In fact, prayer is nothing else than an uplifting of our spirit into God. Each Sacrament has its own effect, even though all of them have but one aim and purpose, which is to unite us to God."[8] Most all other Christian religions understand the importance of the prayer part, but it is a shame they completely miss the return part, which is God bestowing His grace back to us through the Sacraments. There is no hoping that I get God's grace, or wondering if I will get grace; God's grace is guaranteed. However, you have to be properly disposed (meaning in a state of grace, unaware of any grave sin on your soul) to fully receive that grace and make it effective.

The Quickest, Easiest, Surest Way

What makes you as a Catholic so special? What makes you deserve this? Nothing. We don't deserve to be born, and yet we're born again when we're baptized. We don't deserve the bread we eat, and yet we are given the Bread of Life in the Eucharist. We are given all this — and more — in the Sacraments. Consider the parable in Matthew 20:1-16, where Jesus talks about the laborers in the vineyard who worked all day long. At the end of the day, the owner sent a few other workers into the vineyard for the last hour. Then it came time for him to pay everyone. The way our human mind works, we expected the guy who worked all day to get more money than the guy who only worked the last hour.

Here's what's interesting. The owner paid those guys who worked all day the wage they had agreed on. He did not cheat them. Now here comes these other few people who worked just the last hour, and the owner decided to pay them a full wage. And the first workers understandably got angry because it seems unfair that both groups got the same wages. Basically, the owner of the vineyard is saying, "Is it not lawful for me to do what I wish with my own money? Did I cheat you? No. I gave you the amount of money we agreed on, but I wish to give these men, although they've only worked an hour, this extra grace. Sorry if you don't like it, but I have the right to do that." This reply scandalizes our sense of economic justice, but it fits the nature of the world, and it is the world of nature (God's creation) rather than economics or politics (man's creation) that declares the glory of God. The Sacraments declare the same "scandalous" generosity offered to the laborers who only worked one hour. It can seem unfair that Catholics are given all this extra sacramental help — this extra *easier* grace, so to speak — to get to Heaven. We don't deserve to be born, or to be born again, in Baptism. We don't deserve God's sun, or God's Son, who redeemed us 2,000 years ago and then gave us the Sacraments to continue receiving this grace today. We don't deserve delicious bread and wine, or the Body and Blood of Christ, but as Catholics, we are given all this (and more). Don't waste it! It's kind of like — the easy way! Yes, that's actually what the Sacraments are: the extra boost we need to become saints and get us to Heaven. Amazing.

Your Soul is Marked Forever

Of the seven Sacraments, three are primary, and they're what we call indelible, meaning you can't repeat them. They're only done once in your life, because an indelible mark is put on your soul by the Holy Spirit, which God will recognize at our judgment. Baptism puts an indelible mark on your soul. Confirmation puts an indelible mark on your soul. And Holy Orders puts an indelible mark on the priest's (and deacon's) soul. Differently, the other Sacraments can be repeated. Jesus says marriage is forever, but if a spouse dies or if there are grounds for annulment, marriage can be repeated. Catholics are encouraged to make generous use of the Eucharist on a regular basis (provided you are in a state of grace), Reconciliation on a regular basis (especially if you are aware of grave sin), and Anointing of the Sick when needed.

Your parish offers preparation classes for Baptism to parents and godparents. Children are usually prepared for First Holy Communion and Confirmation, with their sponsors, in parish religious education classes, or in Catholic school. Adults can prepare for the three Sacraments of Initiation through the Order of Christian Initiation of Adults (OCIA, formerly RCIA) program in their parish. And to be married in the Catholic Church, the engaged couple will work with their priest for several weeks on marriage preparation, usually called Pre-Cana. Holy Orders, of course, is part of an extensive formation program run by a diocese or a religious order to ordain men to the priesthood.

This book is not intended to be the last word on the seven Sacraments — far from it. Instead, consider it a primer or refresher, to rekindle a desire for learning more about these wondrous gifts of our Catholic faith. The best place for further reading is the *Catechism of the Catholic Church*. And always remember, your parish priest is by nature a teacher of the faith, and eager to answer your questions. I know I am, so let's get started!

THE SACRAMENTS OF INITIATION

Baptism

> Holy Baptism is the basis of the whole Christian life, the gateway to life in the Spirit (*vitae spiritualis ianua*), and the door which gives access to the other sacraments. Through Baptism we are freed from sin and reborn as sons of God; we become members of Christ, are incorporated into the Church and made sharers in her mission: "Baptism is the sacrament of regeneration through water and in the word."
>
> — *Catechism of the Catholic Church*, 1213

At one time or another, we have all been asked, "Are you saved?" Until recently, I never really knew how to answer this question. Yes, of course, I know Jesus. But now I respond, "Yes, I've been baptized 'in the name of the Father, and of the Son, and of the Holy Spirit.' I have been saved through the Sacrament of Baptism, and as long as I stay true to those vows of Baptism and living my Christian faith, I will have eternal life." It's as simple as that. To "baptize" means to "immerse," but not just in water — the one who is baptized is immersed into the death of Christ and rises with Him in new life (see 2 Cor 5:17). Jesus said, "Amen, amen, I say to you, no one can enter the kingdom of God without being born of water and Spirit" (Jn 3:5). [9] Baptism is the *true* born-again experience.

In the Old Testament, Baptism was prefigured. Water was seen as a source of life and death in the desert (since everyone needs water to live). God spared Noah and the ark from the devastating waters of the flood. The parting of the Red Sea allowed Israel to be free from the slavery of Egypt, crossing the water to find the Promised Land, eternal life. But we don't all need to go to the Middle East and dunk ourselves in the Jordan River to be saved, because we have Jesus Christ in the Sacraments. At the beginning of His public life, Jesus was baptized in the Jordan. And at the end of His life on the Cross, what came forth from His side? Blood and Water. Again, this water was a sign of Baptism.

Do you ever wonder why some people talk about Baptism being a death? Water can give life, but it also can kill if you drown. Water at Baptism drowns your sins. The Holy Spirit kills sin within us in Baptism. It drowns out sin and gives us life in Christ. The one who is baptized is immersed into the death of Christ and rises with Him as a "new creation" (2 Cor 5:17). As we used to say in Mass before the retranslation of 2011, "Dying you destroyed our death, rising you restored our life." Our death (drowning) is now followed by a resurrection to life, like Noah.

Remember the Great Commission: Jesus said, "Go, therefore, and make disciples of all nations, baptizing them in the name of the Father, and of the Son, and of the holy Spirit" (Mt 28:19). Jesus instructed this because He said Baptism is necessary for salvation (at least for all those to whom the Gospel has been proclaimed and who have had the possibility of asking for it). Baptism makes us adopted children of God and heirs to Heaven, and also initiates us into the Catholic Church and grants us access to the rest of the Sacraments.

Form, Matter, Minister

What does a Sacrament require? First of all, a Sacrament needs a minister who intends to confect the Sacrament. The Host is *only* the Eucharist (the Body of Christ) if the priest intends to consecrate it with specific words. But Sacraments are not magic spells; rather, they are moments in which God grants the privilege of allowing us to be part of His plan to deliver grace. Sleepwalking while pouring water on someone and saying the formula for Baptism is *not* a valid Baptism. However, the priest saying the proper formula given in the rite of the Sacrament is an instrumental channel of grace for the recipient. It is the way God has given us — remember that all seven Sacraments are in the Bible — to receive actual grace.

Now, in addition to the intention of the priest (*minister*), the minimum factors that are needed for a Sacrament to be valid are referred to as "form" and "matter." These would be the *how* and *what* of the Sacrament. *Form* is what is said and done during the rite, and *matter* is whatever material thing is required to be present during the Sacrament. Not everything that normally occurs in a Sacrament is required, however. For example, some parts of the Baptism rites whose symbolism is important to what is going on (the candle, white gown, etc.) do not constitute sacramental matter because the Sacrament is still valid in their absence.

Baptism, like all Sacraments, has these three elements that give it its unique character. The *matter* is the physical sign, water. Nothing can live without water, and our souls need the water of Baptism to live, to have eternal life. This water is also a sign of the cleansing of our souls of original sin, in God's mercy. The *minister* of Baptism is a priest, deacon, or bishop. The *form*, or ritual, is simply the words that are spoken during a Sacrament. The words "I baptize you in the name of the Father, and of the Son, and of the Holy Spirit" (the *form*) are spoken at Baptism, as water (the *matter*) is poured on the forehead three times, one for each of the Persons of the Trinity, by the priest or deacon. This is called the trinitarian formula and must be said exactly, or the Baptism is invalid.

The Church also accepts the immersion or dunking of a baby (or adult) three times in water, but that's not required.

Anointing with sacred chrism (oil mixed with balsam and consecrated by a bishop) on the forehead in the shape of a cross is done by the priest or deacon. (As mentioned, candles and a white christening gown are wonderful additions to the ceremony, but not necessary.) The Catholic Church considers that all Baptisms performed in this manner are valid Catholic Baptisms, even if performed in another Christian church.

It's important, when possible, to conduct a Baptism in a church with a priest or deacon, so that there is a formal record. This record is very important so that the other Sacraments can be administered in the future. At least one godparent is required, someone who is at least 16 years old and a fully initiated (baptized and confirmed) practicing Catholic in good standing (a letter from the candidate's pastor can attest to this). Choose your godparent(s) wisely: The godparent is someone who will pray for your child and teach him or her by word and example to be a good Catholic. Forget what you see in those *Godfather* movies — a good godparent will be a lifelong spiritual companion and inspiration. It takes a village, according to the *Catechism*:

> For the grace of Baptism to unfold, the parents' help is important. So too is the role of the *godfather* and *godmother*, who must be firm believers, able and ready to help the newly baptized — child or adult — on the road of Christian life. Their task is a truly ecclesial function (*officium*). The whole ecclesial community bears some responsibility for the development and safeguarding of the grace given at Baptism (1255).

Everyone who is to be baptized is required to make a profession of faith. This is done personally in the case of an adult or by the parents and by the Church in the case of infants.

Did you know that, in an emergency, anyone can baptize? Imagine that you, a layperson, witness a car accident where someone has been seriously injured and an ambulance is on its way. If this person is still conscious but gravely wounded, a good question to ask is, "Are you baptized?" If the answer is no, then with their permission, you may baptize them according to the matter and form above. In the same way, parents can baptize a dying baby in the case of emergency if a priest is not present. (Incidentally, if the only water that can be found in an emergency is dirty, say from a puddle or ditch, it can be used as it is water. However, spit or saliva is *not* allowed as it is not "true water" — Pope Innocent III ruled on that in 1206.[10]) Also, please keep in mind that although anyone can baptize under certain circumstances, that does not mean you as a grandmother can baptize your grandbabies in the bathtub while their parents are at work! In cases of non-emergencies, the permission of at least one parent is required, and the Baptism should be done formally at the parish as we've said.

Why bother to baptize? In addition to washing away original sin, Jesus said it is necessary to enter into eternal life. And the Catholic Church says it is necessary to enter into the Mystical Body of Christ, which is the Catholic Church. God, however, is not bound by the Sacraments and can perform this same cleansing of the soul through other extraordinary means if He so chooses. These are known as a Baptism of Blood and Baptism of Desire. Baptism of Blood occurs when a person who has not been baptized by water (using the proper form) is martyred for their faith in Jesus Christ. Baptism of Desire is when a person, through no fault of their own, has never heard of Jesus Christ or His message. Upon that person's death, God can decide to dispense His grace, judging them by their actions, and if they would have wished for Baptism had they known of its importance. Baptism of Desire can also happen when someone is a catechumen, preparing for Baptism, but died before having had the chance to receive this Sacrament.

Effects of Baptism

Baptism wipes away the original sin that all of us received at conception, as well as all sin and punishment for people above the age of reason. (Note: This is why Divine Mercy Sunday is often referred to as *like* a "second baptism," because it wipes away all sin and punishment. For more information on the Extraordinary Promise of Jesus, please see my book *Understanding Divine Mercy*.[11]) Because of the grace of Baptism, it makes the person a participant in the divine life of the Trinity through the grace of justification, which incorporates one into Christ and into the Church. Grace is not just receiving knowledge of God, but receiving God Himself in us. The highest good in all the universe is grace, the grace of Divine Sonship, and this is the meaning and purpose of Baptism. As a result, when you are baptized, you share in the three offices of Christ: Priest, Prophet, and King.

Are you a priest? No, you're not a *ministerial* priest like I am (as I received the Sacrament of Holy Orders), but by virtue of your Baptism, you share in the *common* (or *royal*) priesthood of Christ. When you go to Mass, for example, you share in the Sacrifice of the Mass along with the priest. When you pray the Chaplet of Divine Mercy, you are offering a sacrifice, similar to the second part of the Mass, the Liturgy of the Eucharist. Together we share in communion with the Body of Christ, which is important, because that's what Heaven is! Baptism here on earth is preparing us for Heaven, because Baptism bestows upon us the theological virtues of faith, hope, and charity, which enable us to live a holy life. Those virtues don't come on their own. They only come to us through Baptism, planted like seeds in the soil of the soul, waiting to germinate later. Through living the Christian life with the help of divine grace, those seeds come to fruition and enable us to be ready for life in the heavenly Kingdom.

Are you a prophet? A prophet teaches. Through the grace of Baptism and the Sacraments, we are commanded to go forth and bring Christ to the world, our families, our workplace, and the secular culture. That's evangelization. You are expected to be a teacher, sharing your faith with others. The *Catechism* reminds us, "Lay believers are in the front line of Church life; for them the Church is the animating principle of human society. Therefore, they in particular ought to have an ever-clearer consciousness not only of belonging to the Church, but of being the Church" (899).

And are you a king? A king governs. You are to govern your body, your soul, your family, and so on, in holiness. It's about exercising leadership. Ask yourself, *How can I make the world more holy? Do I stand up for our faith? Do I exercise my right to vote properly, electing officials who will uphold the dignity of all human life?* Our efforts, Vatican II noted, "will imbue culture and human activity with genuine moral values; they will better prepare the field of the world for the seed of the Word of God; and at the same time they will open wider the doors of the Church by which the message of peace may enter the world."[12]

Indelible Mark

When you make the Sign of the Cross, you're branding yourself as a Christian. Like a cowboy who brands his cattle so that others will know the cattle belong to that cowboy, with the Sign of the Cross you are now branded to show you belong to God when the angels come on the last day to separate the wheat from the chaff. "His winnowing fork is in his hand, and he will clear his threshing floor and will gather his wheat into the granary; but the chaff he will burn with unquenchable fire" (Mt 3:12). It's the same with Baptism: When you are baptized you receive the Holy Spirit, an ontological change happens, and an indelible mark is put on your soul. Your soul has changed and now belongs forever to Jesus. Again, amazing.

Baptism confers the first sanctifying grace because it washes away original sin, something we need to do as soon as possible in the lives of our loved ones. We baptize infants (preferably within one month of their birth) as they're born with this sin and need to be freed from the evil one. It offers the freedom that belongs to the children of God and is a sign that you're in God's family now — and nothing can change that.

When I was 7 years old, I announced I wanted a new family, mainly because I thought my mother and father were playing favorites, neglecting me in favor of my only sibling. In a comical but loving way, my mother actually helped me draft a letter to the local newspaper to place an ad to find a new family. My dad saw what I was doing and said, "Huh? You can't change the family God put you into!" and he walked away after eating the pile of peanuts I had so diligently worked on shelling during the discussion with my mother. Unbeknownst to me, he was teaching me some of the hard realities of life. It wasn't too many years later that I saw the wisdom in his words: You can't change the family God put you into. In a similar way, Baptism puts us into God's family, and not even Satan can change that. We are now in a family, the Body of Christ, that gives us the Sacraments. All of the people there were put there by God through Baptism, and even we can't change that about ourselves.

Some people say, "I want to let my kids decide for themselves when they get older whether they will be baptized and members of the Church or not." But do those people say the same thing about what their children eat for supper? Would you say, "I am not going to require my kids to eat their vegetables. I am going to let them decide for themselves when they get older whether they want to eat vegetables or not." Of course not. As a parent you know what is best for your children: that your kids need bodily nourishment even before they are old enough to understand the importance of nourishment. It is the legal and God-given right of the parents to speak on behalf of their children during their infancy and even into their adolescence. The same is true for the souls of your children, which need nourishment as well, right from the start, even before they know what's good for them. They can always choose to accept or reject the Church when they get older. But until they are old enough to decide that for themselves, don't starve them of the spiritual nourishment that they need!

Remember John 15:16: "You did not choose me but I chose you. And I appointed you to go and bear fruit, fruit that will last, so that the Father will give you whatever you ask him in my name." God knows each of us by name. In Baptism, a Christian receives his or her name, initiating us into God's family via the Church, which will lead us to salvation. Saint Peter says, Baptism "now saves you — not as a removal of dirt from the body, but as an appeal to God for a good conscience, through the resurrection of Jesus Christ, who has gone into heaven and is at the right hand of God, with angels, authorities, and powers made subject to him" (1 Pet 3:21-22). What a beautiful family to be a part of!

(Infant) Baptism in Scripture and Tradition

The origins of Baptism are found in Scripture. In the Old Testament, if a man was to become a Jew, he had to believe in the God of Israel and be circumcised. Infants were initiated into the Jewish faith through circumcision at only 8 days old. Then, in the New Testament, if you became a Christian, you had to believe in Jesus and be baptized. In Mark's Gospel we learn:

> John [the] Baptist appeared in the desert proclaiming a baptism of repentance for the forgiveness of

sins. People of the whole Judean countryside and all the inhabitants of Jerusalem were going out to him and were being baptized by him in the Jordan River as they acknowledged their sins. ... And this is what he proclaimed: "One mightier than I is coming after me. I am not worthy to stoop and loosen the thongs of his sandals. I have baptized you with water; he will baptize you with the holy Spirit" (Mk 1:4-5, 7-8).[13]

Jesus' first public act was to be baptized by John (of course, Jesus was without sin and so did not need the forgiveness of sins; His Baptism sanctified the waters and anticipated His victory over sin and death).

Saying more on the topic of infants, Luke tells us that "they were bringing even infants" to Jesus, and He Himself related this to the kingdom of God: "Let the children come to me, and do not stop them, for it is to such as these that the kingdom of God belongs" (Lk 18:15-16). Many Fundamentalists reject infant Baptism, saying one needs the "born again" experience, and this cannot happen until a certain level of maturity is reached. They say you have to be old enough to make the choice and accept Jesus as Lord and Savior, and then get baptized. The problem is, for them Baptism is simply a sign of conversion; it's not a Sacrament and it does not convey grace to the soul.

But did you know the age of reason for children is only 7? As such, after age 7 there's some responsibility, even for a child, for the actions they choose to do. Do you want to be responsible for not aiding your child with the grace he or she needs not to die with sin on their soul, even at such a young age? You might say, "Oh, but they are only a child." Well, I know that by the time I was 7, I knew right from wrong. I knew it was wrong to steal or cheat; I knew you were to share and not be uncharitable to others, or abuse animals. Why would you not free a beautiful little child from the grip of the original sin that is the source of the concupiscence (inclination to sin) that leads to those personal sins? Who wouldn't want to wash their child clean of sin? Well, if you don't baptize your child, you're leaving them quite dirty with the stain of original sin. As mentioned earlier, they need to be freed from the power of the evil one and brought into that realm of freedom that belongs to the children of God.

The Church Fathers certainly believed this. Saint Irenaeus wrote in A.D. 189, "He [Jesus] came to save all through himself; all, I say, who through him are reborn in God: infants, and children, and youths, and old men."[14] In A.D. 388, St. John Chrysostom wrote, "You see how many are the benefits of baptism, and some think its heavenly grace consists only in the remission of sins, but we have enumerated ten honors [it bestows]! For this reason we baptize even infants, though they are not defiled by [personal] sins, so that there may be given to them holiness, righteousness, adoption, inheritance, brotherhood with Christ, and that they may be his [Christ's] members."[15] Saint Augustine noted in A.D. 408, "The custom of Mother Church in baptizing infants is certainly not to be scorned, nor is it to be regarded in any way as superfluous, nor is it to be believed that its tradition is anything except apostolic,"[16] meaning the practice came straight from the apostles. In the 13th century, St. Thomas Aquinas cited Augustine and other Church Fathers in supporting infant Baptism: "Children, like adults, are made members of Christ in Baptism; hence they must, of necessity, receive an influx of grace and virtues from the Head."[17]

The Catholic Church does what it does today regarding infant Baptism because it has been a tradition in the Church for almost 2,000 years. It's amazing to me how so many non-Catholics ignore this fact, supported by historical writings, by claiming the Catholic position on this matter has no basis in Scripture. Although it is based in Scripture (see the passages below), our faith is based on both Scripture *and*

Tradition, as St. Paul tells us in 2 Thessalonians 2:15: "So then, brothers and sisters, stand firm and hold fast to the traditions that you were taught by us, either by word of mouth or by our letter." How do you just ignore that the Church Fathers in the Apostolic Tradition say to baptize the little children? No Christian objections to this practice were ever voiced until the Reformation, and after. And there should not have been an objection because, as we said, infant Baptism is supported in the Bible.

Recall that in the Acts of the Apostles, when Paul and Silas were imprisoned, a violent earthquake gave everyone a chance to flee, but Paul and Silas and all the prisoners remained, much to the astonishment of the jailer:

> Paul shouted in a loud voice, "Do not harm yourself, for we are all here." The jailer called for lights, and rushing in, he fell down trembling before Paul and Silas. Then he brought them outside and said, "Sirs, what must I do to be saved?" They answered, "Believe on the Lord Jesus, and you will be saved, you and your household." They spoke the word of the Lord to him and to all who were in his house. At the same hour of the night he took them and washed their wounds; then he and his entire family were baptized without delay. He brought them up into the house and set food before them; and he and his entire household rejoiced that he had become a believer in God (Acts 16:28-34).

As the concept of the "household" would include children and infants, we can say that the jailer's entire family was baptized. And Paul replied in his First Letter to the Corinthians that he baptized "the household of Stephanas" (1 Cor 1:16). Wouldn't "the household" have included children and infants? Why would they be excluded? In the Acts of the Apostles, the people of Jerusalem, upon hearing Peter's words, "were cut to the heart and said to Peter and to the other Apostles, 'Brothers, what should we do?' Peter said to them, 'Repent, and be baptized every one of you in the name of Jesus Christ so that your sins may be forgiven; and you will receive the gift of the Holy Spirit. For the promise is for you, for your children, and for all who are far away, everyone whom the Lord our God calls to him'" (Acts 2:37-39). So there's a biblical answer for so-called "crazy Catholics" who baptize children not old enough to make a choice: St. Peter said, "The promise is for you, for your children."

Another compelling argument for infant Baptism is found by comparing it to infant circumcision in the Old Testament. Those born as Jews were circumcised in anticipation of the Jewish faith in which they would be raised. Similarly, those born in Christian households were to be baptized in anticipation of the Christian faith in which they would be raised. As a result, Paul notes that Baptism has replaced circumcision (see Col 2:11-12). Circumcision of adults was rare, since there were few converts to Judaism, so if Paul meant to exclude infants, he would not have chosen circumcision as a comparison.

Other skeptics of infant Baptism point out that God would not deny Heaven to an unbaptized infant. Catholics would not disagree on this point, because while *we* are not above the Sacraments, *God* is, so His infinite mercy is a big reason we have hope for the salvation of these babies. This also brings up the question of limbo and children who die before Baptism. First of all, limbo is not official Church teaching. We believe that infants who die without Baptism may be saved and brought to eternal happiness because they are under the age of reason (age 7). They could not have made a decision for Christ; they were infants. It is the same for healthy newborn babies, but their parents and godparents made the decision for Christ on their behalf, so children who die suddenly are protected by God's same grace promised in Baptism. This brings to mind one of my favorite statements on the subject, coming from *The Apostolic Tradition* (A.D. 215): "Baptize first the children, and if they can speak for themselves let them do so. Otherwise, let their parents or other relatives speak for them."[18]

Others will point to the Holy Innocents who died unexpectedly, stating that these infants didn't need Baptism to gain eternal life. They will say, "Do you think the Holy Innocents, those little children murdered so that the Infant Christ could flee, are not going to have eternal reward? Of course they will." Again, God's grace is not bound solely to His Sacraments, but we are bound to seek it where He has promised to provide it. Yes, in the case of the Holy Innocents, God can give the grace of Baptism without the actual Sacrament being conferred, and in that case He surely did. But don't take that risk. All salvation comes from Christ, and therefore, in some way, through His Body, the Church. Baptism shows the way.

One final point that most everyone has pondered at one time or another, is, *Why is the world in such a mess today? Why does the world seem so much more sinful than it was even when we were kids?* I have a theory that no one has yet disagreed with. I personally believe that it is because we are not baptizing our babies. We explained earlier that only in Baptism do we receive the *supernatural* virtues of faith, hope, and love. Yes, we can have these same virtues on the *natural* level without Baptism, such as me having a love for Detroit Lions football, or a parent having faith that their child will pass an exam, or a lonely person hoping they can meet the perfect friend. These virtues are good, but they are not on a supernatural level. To truly love like Christ, for example, we need the *supernatural* virtue of love. Thus, without baptizing our children, we are denying them these virtues that truly enable them to live Christian life to the fullest.

Think about this. World leaders today average in age from their mid-40s to 60 years of age. That means they were born between 1965 and 1980, the exact time (post-Vatican II) that Church attendance plummeted and the importance of the faith in people's lives waned considerably. Now these children have grown up and are the world's leaders, but they are taking on this herculean task without the supernatural virtues needed to do it. Instead of having faith, atheism in this post-Christian world has greatly increased. Instead of having hope, there is more despair than I can ever remember seeing in the world. It seems almost everyone today is on some kind of antidepressant or other drug to affect their emotional mood. Instead of experiencing true love, we see hatred control people's lives. Yes, we are in a mess, and again I believe it goes directly back to apathy toward the Sacraments — in this case, Baptism. I cannot stress strongly enough that not baptizing our infants is a huge mistake, perhaps mankind's biggest mistake of all.

Confirmation

> It must be explained to the faithful that the reception of the sacrament of Confirmation is necessary for the completion of baptismal grace. For "by the sacrament of Confirmation, [the baptized] are more perfectly bound to the Church and are enriched with a special strength of the Holy Spirit. Hence they are, as true witnesses of Christ, more strictly obliged to spread and defend the faith by word and deed."
>
> — *Catechism of the Catholic Church*, 1285

Do you know that Baptism by itself is incomplete? The *Catechism* states, "Every baptized person not yet confirmed can and should receive the Sacrament of Confirmation" (1306). Few people know that Confirmation completes and strengthens Baptism. Confirmation brings a "confirming" or deepening of baptismal grace — hence its name. Being baptized is absolutely necessary to begin your life, as it is a Sacrament of our *new* birth (our first birth was stained by original sin), but it's not enough to complete it. Confirmation gives us a greater conformity to Christ that expands on Baptism, so the glory of our sonship with God can be lived out morally better at a time when we are most facing temptations and a pagan culture. Saint John Henry Newman held that "Confirmation seals in their fullness, winds up and consigns, completes the entire round of those sanctifying gifts which are begun, which are given inchoately in Baptism."[19]

I like to call Confirmation the *Sacrament of Battle*, where you become a soldier of Christ. In a way, you become an "adult" in the faith, which is not dependent upon your age (and perhaps that's why the age of Confirmation varies so greatly around the world). I also feel that Confirmation is the most underrated of all the seven Sacraments and often overlooked. And yet it increases the seven gifts of the Holy Spirit received at Baptism — wisdom, understanding, counsel, fortitude, knowledge, piety, and fear of the Lord (or, as some call it, awe and wonder) — that allow us to fight this battle and be victorious. We don't have a prayer of winning this battle and finding salvation if we are not armed with these spiritual weapons. At Confirmation these gifts of the Holy Spirit are strengthened in the soul, and it gives the recipient the power to overcome occasions of sin and rise to a new level of holiness. Let's look at these incredibly important gifts in more detail.

Gifts and Fruits of the Holy Spirit

If Baptism is like a seed of divine life in the soul, then Confirmation makes that seed bloom. If Baptism is the Sacrament of *birth* into divine life, then Confirmation is the Sacrament of *maturity*. It pours into our souls the power of the Holy Spirit and strengthens the seven gifts just as the apostles experienced at Pentecost. The prophet Isaiah (see 11:1-2) describes these seven gifts, as does the *Catechism*, which states that the gifts are "permanent dispositions which make man docile in following the promptings of the Holy Spirit" (1830). We lose them only when we lose the state of grace in our soul through mortal sin. They sustain the moral life, they perfect the virtues (we need the gifts to live a virtuous life), and they allow us to become students of the Spirit. The seven gifts of the Holy Spirit, given at Baptism and strengthened at Confirmation, as we said, are our spiritual weaponry for the spiritual warfare of everyday life. They are as follows:

Wisdom. The first and greatest gift. It allows us to see things in our lives and things of the world from the way God sees them. It is the opposite of the worldly view. Wisdom is being able to see God everywhere and in every situation. Jesus is Wisdom Himself.

Understanding. In understanding we comprehend how we need to live as a follower of Christ. It is knowing what it takes to be a disciple, but also to be open and aware to how others think and feel, like having compassion for others. You have empathy; you have understanding for them.

Counsel. This is supernatural intuition. It helps a person judge correctly between right and wrong. We can make good decisions and decisions to avoid sin. Because we are living it, we can give good advice.

Fortitude. Courage — standing up for what is right in the eyes of God even in the face of suffering or rejection. Fortitude allows one to resist fear and overcome obstacles by being strong, even if facing martyrdom.

Knowledge. We come to know our faith and teachings of the Church so that we know the meaning of God, not just information about Him. Knowledge is the gift to be able to study and learn.

Piety. This is reverence. We have a deep sense of respect for God and the Church. We recognize our reliance on God; we worship and obey God as our Father, growing in personal holiness.

Fear of the Lord. This is awe and wonder as we are made aware of the glory of God and the fear associated with separating ourselves from God. The fear is more *filial* (fear of offending) than *servile* (fear of punishment). Fear of the Lord is the beginning of wisdom.

The *fruits of the Holy Spirit*, on the other hand, are the effects in us of living a life of holiness, according to the Spirit. The *Catechism* describes them as "perfections that the Holy Spirit forms in us as the first fruits of eternal glory" (1832). Although the Greek New Testament lists nine fruits (see Gal 5:22-23), Christian tradition, following St. Jerome, has given us 12: charity, joy, peace, patience, kindness, goodness, generosity, gentleness, faithfulness, modesty, self-control, and chastity. Let's look at each.

Charity. Thanks to the Holy Spirit, we are infused with the capacity for love — love of God and our neighbor. This is a selfless love, without the desire for reward.

Joy. Internal joy is better than external happiness. I will be happy if my football team wins the Super Bowl, but that will not bring true joy. The Holy Spirit makes us realize that true joy comes not from things such as money or possessions, but from knowing and following Jesus. Our joy is that someday we will be with Him in Heaven.

Peace. Not lack of war but feeling good in your conscience. Christ didn't bring peace but the sword. When we rely on God, a tranquility dwells in our soul. We experience that inner peace through prayer and worship and, in turn, work to build a peaceful world, especially in our hearts.

Patience. Here's the fruit I am often lacking! But showing patience and kindness to others reinforces our understanding of God's mercy toward others and His forgiveness. As St. Paul wrote, "Love is patient; love is kind" (1 Cor 13:4). It is bearing the faults of others.

Kindness. Doing good things for others. Sometimes called "benignity," this fruit is part of the Golden Rule, or as Jesus taught us, "Do to others as you would have them do to you" (Lk 6:31).

Goodness. This is purity of intention. We don't do good things just to get recognized, but because the act is good in and of itself. Embracing goodness means renouncing evil, repenting our sins, and always striving to do God's will.

Generosity. Generosity is not simply confined to sharing your worldly goods; it's also about being generous with your time and talents with your neighbor, and making time in your life for God and accepting His generosity.

Gentleness. This is acting lovingly. It happens to the best of us: we lose our temper when confronted by an angry, vengeful person. But the Holy Spirit inspires us to control our emotions and behavior, mindful of the need to show forgiveness and love toward others.

Faithfulness. With the help of the grace of the Holy Spirit, we strive to be faithful to the teachings of Jesus Christ, the Holy Scriptures, and the Catholic Church, and live our lives according to God's directives.

Modesty. We often focus on our outward appearance, which may be important, but it cannot be our primary focus. Modesty also goes hand in hand with humility and being pure in our thoughts and hearts.

Self-control. This is controlling the passions. The ancient Greeks called it *medem agan* (nothing in excess). It's about controlling your appetites and avoiding indulgence of things both sinful and not sinful.

Chastity. This is self-control with our gift of sexuality. As a Catholic priest, I have given myself completely to God and embrace celibacy. Chastity for the laity means abstaining from sexual activity prior to marriage, and remaining faithful and respectful to your spouse within marriage.

So, the fruits of the Holy Spirit are the good habits, the good deeds that come from living as a child of God. And the gifts of the Holy Spirit, when used rightly, bear good fruit! For example, the *gift* of fear of the Lord leads to the *fruit* of chastity; the *gift* of counsel leads to the *fruit* of faithfulness. When a confirmed person cooperates with the graces that the Holy Spirit provides, the person makes spiritual headway — willing to listen to and obey the promptings of the Spirit — and bears fruit. To summarize, all who are confirmed are equipped with the gifts of the Holy Spirit to live a virtuous and holy life, and the confirmed are sent forth to bear fruit for the benefit of the Church and world. Use the gifts!

Form, Matter, Minister

The *minister* of Confirmation is typically a bishop; however, on special occasions when a bishop is not available, a priest may administer Confirmation with permission. The *matter* of Confirmation is sacred chrism, which is the oil that the bishop places on the recipient's forehead in the shape of the cross. The *form* is the words of the bishop: "Be sealed with the gifts of the Holy Spirit." Why do we use sacred chrism in Confirmation, as we do in Baptism? Because it follows the tradition of being anointed in Scripture. In the

Bible, if someone is anointed with oil, it meant that person had a Spirit-led mission; moreover, the anointing with oil signified the Holy Spirit descending on the person. The name "Christ" is not Jesus' last name. It means "Messiah" — *Christos* in Greek, which means "the anointed one." As Jesus was anointed for a mission, a confirmed Christian is literally an anointed one who is given a Spirit-led mission. What's your mission? To paraphrase the *Baltimore Catechism*, we are to know, love, and serve our Lord in this life, and thereby prepare ourselves, our family, and everyone we meet for eternal life in Heaven. Amen!

Oil was a strengthening element in the ancient world, and the Church has carried on that tradition. If you seal something with oil, the object becomes stronger. A container, for instance, is less likely to leak. If you seal a wound with oil, it heals. Athletes used to be given oil to soothe their muscles to help them compete better. So the seal with sacred chrism at Confirmation shows that we are now stronger. It also shows we belong to God, as an indelible mark is put on our soul. As I have said, it's like branding yourself so that, at the end of time when souls are separated — the wheat from the chaff, the good from the bad — the angels will carry yours to the Lord.

According to Canon law, the Sacrament of Confirmation should be conferred in church, during Mass, and a sponsor is required. Like a godparent in Baptism, a sponsor in Confirmation is to be a practicing Catholic in good standing (attested by his parish) and someone you know well and respect. The sponsor takes on the role of a spiritual parent who "brings the candidate to receive the sacrament, presents him to the minister for the anointing, and will later help him to fulfill his baptismal promises faithfully under the influence of the Holy Spirit."[20] Being a sponsor is a lifelong commitment. My Confirmation sponsor was Tom Eby of Monroe, Michigan (God rest his soul). He was the quintessential All-American young man who was athletic, handsome, and most of all a man of God. His father and my father were life-long friends, played football together, and were solid Christians. As Tom did for me, your Confirmation sponsor should take you under their wing, teach you the faith, and walk with you in your faith journey. Don't take it lightly: choose your sponsor wisely.

Taking a saint's name at Confirmation adopts the saint as a special heavenly patron, or honors a saint to whom one has a special devotion. It also gives the candidate the chance to understand, and learn to rely upon, the Communion of Saints. I chose Francis as my Confirmation name, after St. Francis of Assisi. To me, as an eighth-grader, he was a cool and fearless guy who loved animals, as I did. While the practice is still in use today, some dioceses have encouraged returning to the older tradition of not picking a new name at Confirmation. The idea is that the person is already supposed to have a Christian name, given to him in Baptism, and continuing to use that name at Confirmation will serve as a link between these two Sacraments of Christian Initiation.[21] In some ways I may disagree, especially when so many Christian kids today are not given the name of a saint at birth. For every Joseph there are at least three Jacksons, and for every Mary, there are several Madisons. And some names are just random compilations, with no spiritual meaning at all.

Confirmation in the Bible

Let's look at the Sacrament of Confirmation in Scripture, and the reception of the Holy Spirit:

> Now when the apostles at Jerusalem heard that Samaria had accepted the word of God, they sent Peter and John to them. The two went down and prayed for them that they might receive the Holy Spirit (for as yet the Spirit had not come upon any of them; they had only been baptized in the name of the Lord Jesus). Then Peter and John laid their

hands on them, and they received the Holy Spirit (Acts 8:14-17).

And St. Paul writes in the Letter to the Ephesians:

> Let no evil talk come out of your mouths, but only what is useful for building up, as there is need, so that your words may give grace to those who hear. And do not grieve the Holy Spirit of God, with which you were marked with a seal for the day of redemption. Put away from you all bitterness and wrath and anger and wrangling and slander, together with all malice, and be kind to one another, tenderhearted, forgiving one another, as God in Christ has forgiven you. (Eph 4:29-32)

To be sealed with the Holy Spirit in Confirmation means we are given the grace to cooperate with God's grace on the life-long journey to Heaven. If we do not cooperate with the grace of the Sacrament and reject those graces, we risk our soul being lost. It's kind of like putting gas in your tank but not starting the car. The car will go nowhere, even though the tank is full. We must walk the path of conversion and work out our salvation daily.

The Sacrament of Confirmation gives us the special strength of the Holy Spirit to spread and defend the faith as the apostles did. Confirmation could be described as our own personal Pentecost, because at Pentecost, 50 days after Easter, the Holy Spirit came down upon Mary and the apostles. The Holy Spirit does the same thing to you at Confirmation. After all, the apostles were bold and fearless — they went out, they preached about the Lord instead of hiding safely inside. In a way, we are doing this today, even though we may be afraid to mention Jesus in public, even to our family members and close friends. Your own personal Pentecost gives you strength and encouragement, lessening the fear so that you can preach, teach, and live as Christ did. It doesn't mean you have to stand on a soapbox and preach Scripture all day long, but it does mean that, if called upon, you're not afraid to defend God. This is the gift of fortitude, which is strength. Vatican II reminds us of the consequences should we resist such strength in loving as Christ did:

> He is not saved, however, who, though part of the body of the Church, does not persevere in charity. He remains indeed in the bosom of the Church, but, as it were, only in a "bodily" manner and not "in his heart." All the Church's children should remember that their exalted status is to be attributed not to their own merits but to the special grace of Christ. If they fail, moreover, to respond to that grace in thought, word and deed, not only shall they not be saved but they will be the more severely judged.[22]

This is definitely a wake-up call. With Confirmation, we are being drafted into God's "army," the Church. We become soldiers of Christ fighting evil as a full member of the Church. And it doesn't stop at age 15 or 16 — it's a lifetime commitment!

If you ever wonder, *Why can't I be more holy?* or *How can I be holy?* — ask yourself if you are calling upon the gifts of your Confirmation, the gifts of the Holy Spirit. We face hard times right now, and we need the gifts of the Holy Spirit because we can't get by on our own, on our natural virtues, or just "being nice." Those are good, but they're not sufficient. This is why people often say to me when referring to family and friends who don't seem concerned with following God's law, "Well, Father, he doesn't believe in God, but he's a good person." My own aunt once said to me about her coworker, "Oh, well, you know, this person, he's living with his boyfriend and, you know, he doesn't ever go to church or believe in God, but he's really a good person. He donates to charities." Yes, he may be good on the natural level, which is in accord with the earthly values of loving, but that's not enough. You need to reach a supernatural level of virtue, and for that, you need supernatural grace. Natural grace means you're only surviving in this world; you're doing fine in one sense, but you need the supernatural grace from Heaven via the Sacraments if you're going to make it to life eternal.

Confirmation Age

When should you get confirmed? Only those already baptized can receive this Sacrament, and, like Baptism, it can be received only once. Eastern Rite Catholics celebrate Confirmation (and the Eucharist) immediately after Baptism of infants, which is an indication of its importance. Our Western (Latin) Church tradition waits until the candidate has reached the "age of discretion," usually between 7 and 16 years old. I was confirmed at age 14. Saint Thomas Aquinas said, "Age of the body does not determine age of soul. Even in childhood, man can attain spiritual maturity."[23] So look at the spiritual maturity of the candidate to see if they are ready to be confirmed. "Parents and pastors of souls, especially parish priests, are to take care that the faithful are properly instructed to receive the Sacrament and come to it at the appropriate time" (Canon 890). That's the key, because if he or she resists, it may well be better to wait on Confirmation. If a person was confirmed and didn't understand or did not completely believe in the truth and reality of the grace of the Sacrament, the Confirmation may be illicit (done contrary to the law of the Church). It would still be valid, though, and not need to be redone.

Following instruction of candidates in a parish or school program, Confirmation is often conferred between Easter Sunday and Pentecost, and it has to be done before marriage. If you're baptized Catholic, in order to get married in the Catholic Church, you have to be confirmed.

Canon law states that it is the parents' role to see that their children are properly instructed, and Confirmation is part of that instruction. You probably could force your child to be confirmed, but you can't force them to have the proper disposition or openness to receiving those graces flowing into their life and into their hearts. For that to happen, we can only pray and help them prepare their hearts as much as possible. You have the right and obligation as a parent to see that your child is educated in the Catholic faith, just as you have the right and obligation to see that they are educated at school. This way, they are best prepared for life and the life after this life. Thus, if you want to get to Heaven, Confirmation gives you the tools to get there. Don't put it off.

Holy Eucharist

> The holy Eucharist completes Christian initiation. Those who have been raised to the dignity of the royal priesthood by Baptism and configured more deeply to Christ by Confirmation participate with the whole community in the Lord's own sacrifice by means of the Eucharist.
>
> — *Catechism of the Catholic Church*, 1322

Baptism and Confirmation initiate the individual into Christianity, but Holy Eucharist, or Holy Communion, completes this initiation. The Eucharist (from the Greek *eucharistia*, meaning "thanksgiving") connects the person with the rest of the Church at the wedding feast of the Lamb. The medicine for healing all of our ills is the Eucharist — the Body, Blood, Soul, and Divinity of Jesus Christ, the source and summit of our faith. In the Eucharist, over a thousand years before the first non-Catholic Christian religion was even created, St. Ignatius of Antioch said that we "break the one bread that provides the medicine of immortality, the antidote for death and the food that makes us live forever in Jesus Christ."[24]

We hear all the time about the importance of the Eucharist, but we sometimes don't understand why. Well, it's all about mercy. There is nothing the world needs today more than Divine Mercy — as Pope St. John Paul II told us[25] — and there is no greater manifestation of the mercy of God than in the Most Holy Eucharist. Our bodies need food, so it is logical to conclude our souls do as well. That's Holy Communion; it is true soul food. Our Lord leaves His Body and Blood in the form of a Host so He can remain with us until the end of time. In the words of St. Francis de Sales:

> The Savior instituted the most holy Sacrament of the Eucharist, really containing His Body and His Blood, in order that they who eat it might live for ever. ... The most fragile, easily spoilt fruits, such as cherries, apricots, and strawberries, can be kept all the year by being preserved in sugar or honey; so what wonder if our hearts, frail and weakly as they are, are kept from the corruption of sin when they are preserved in the sweetness ("sweeter than honey and the honeycomb") of the Incorruptible Body and Blood of the Son of God. [26]

Saint Faustina refers to the Eucharist throughout her *Diary;* she wrote 16 different prayers in preparation for Holy Communion. In one of the most powerful passages, she said that Jesus told her, "If the angels were capable of envy, they would envy us for two things: one is the receiving of Holy Communion, and the other is suffering."[27] Wow — one thing Catholics don't want anything to do with (suffering) and one thing only 30 percent of Catholics believe in (the Real Presence). These are the two things angels would envy us for! For the most part, we Catholics have no idea what treasures we have, especially in this Sacrament.

Form, Matter, Minister

The *matter* of the Eucharist is unleavened bread, made from wheat, and unspoiled grape wine, into which some water is added. The *minister* is a validly-ordained Catholic priest, and the consecration must take place within the context of the Mass. Only the following words of Jesus Christ, spoken by the priest at the consecration during the Eucharistic Prayer, constitute the *form* of the Eucharist: "Take this, all of you, and eat of it. For this is My Body which will be given up for you." And then, in regard to the Precious Blood: "Take this, all of you, and drink from it. For this is the chalice of My Blood, the Blood of the new and eternal covenant, which will be poured out for you and for many for the forgiveness of sins." The priest concludes, "Do this in memory of Me." Only the bread and wine that the priest intends to consecrate become the Body and Blood of Christ. This is why the priest places the vessels of consecration — the chalice and ciborium — on a small white linen cloth called a corporal (from the Latin *corpus*, meaning "body"; the linen cloth recalls the Shroud of Turin, the burial cloth of Jesus), so there's no doubt what bread and what wine he will consecrate.

One way the Eucharist is different from the other Sacraments is the fact that the priest who consecrates the bread and wine is not necessarily the one who administers the Sacrament to the faithful. Often he is, but due to the practicalities of the number of people at a Mass, or his own health, sometimes there are others to distribute. The ordinary minister of the Eucharist is a bishop, a priest, or a deacon (see Canon 910). The same canon also describes extraordinary ministers: properly-instructed and instituted acolytes or lay faithful who can also assist in the distribution of Communion. But the key word here is "extraordinary," and it should only be used when, Canon law states, "the need of the Church warrants it and ministers are lacking" (230).

What are the fruits of the Eucharist? Holy Communion increases our union with Christ and with His Church. It preserves and renews the life of grace received at Baptism and Confirmation and makes us grow in love for our neighbor. It strengthens us in charity, wipes away venial sins, and preserves us from mortal sin in the future. Can we ask for anything more?

What is the Eucharistic Sacrifice?

The Eucharist is the very sacrifice of Christ Himself. At the Last Supper, Christ instituted the memorial of the Eucharist and entrusted it to the priests — that is why the apostles were present! The Eucharist is a *memorial* in the sense that it makes present and actual for all eternity the sacrifice that Christ offered to the Father on the Cross, once and for all on behalf of mankind. It is not a reenactment — the sacrifice of the Cross and the sacrifice of the Eucharist are *one and the same sacrifice*. The priest and victim are the same; only the manner of offering is different: bloody versus un-bloody. At Mass, the priest is offering the ultimate sacrifice. Remember, we are not re-crucifying Christ; rather, the Mass is a re-presentation of the only one, true Sacrifice of Christ at Calvary. At Mass we are in sacred time; we are really there, at the Crucifixion, as Christ is paying our penalty for sin, which is death. Thus, the Mass is both a meal and a sacrifice. The altar is a table, a table for the meal of the bread and the wine, but it's also the place of sacrifice with Christ's Body and Blood.

Acts of sacrifice have been the essence of religions from the beginning of time. God even commanded it throughout the Bible. The very nature of a sacrificial act requires a priest ordained by God to offer the sacrifice. Not until the 1500s did the Protestants begin to reject the idea of a sacrificial Mass and replace it with ceremonies focused just on prayer and song. That's why, in one sense, there is no such thing as "praise and worship," because to have the fullness of worship you must have sacrifice. While at Calvary, Jesus was the One offering sacrifice and the One being offered; today the One being offered is Christ in the Eucharist and the one offering is the priest *in persona Christi* (in the person of Christ). The Sacrifice of Christ's Body and Blood at Mass makes perfect sense when you view it from the standpoint of Old Testament fulfillment. Leviticus emphasizes the sacredness of blood through priestly sacrifice: "For the life of the flesh is in the blood; and I have given it to you for making atonement for your lives on the altar; for, as life, it is the blood that makes atonement" (Lev 17:11). That is why in Exodus, Moses sprinkled blood on the people to ratify the covenant (Ex 24:8). Now we have the Blood of Christ, which is *precious* because it is Christ's own great ransom paid for the redemption of mankind, the Blood of God made Man shed on the Cross and renewed at every Mass.

Since it came from Christ, one drop was enough to save the whole world from sin. The Precious Blood does it all for us! It ransoms us from death (see Rev 5:9). It frees us from sin, as foreshadowed by the animal sacrifices in the Old Testament (see Heb 9:11-28, 13:12; 1 Jn 1:7; Rev 1:5, 7:14). It redeems and justifies us (see Acts 20:28; Rom 3:25, 5:9; Eph 1:7; 1 Pet 1:18-19). Finally, it reconciles us to God (see Eph 2:13; Col 1:14), equips us for mission (see Heb 13:20-21), and empowers us to conquer Satan (see Rev 12:11). Is that not enough? Saint Faustina implored, "Jesus, do not permit the loss of souls redeemed at so dear a price of Your most precious Blood. O Jesus, when I consider the great price of Your Blood, I rejoice at its immensity, for one drop alone would have been enough for the salvation of all sinners" (*Diary*, 72).

Saint John Chrysostom once said that the angel of death fled when he saw the sacrificed animal blood of the Old Testament priests on the doors of the Jewish people (Passover). How much more will the devil flee, he said, when he sees the true Blood (*not* symbolic animal blood) of the Lamb obtained from the priest on your lips, the doors of your soul?[28] Thus, Jesus chose to institute the Eucharist during a Passover meal, because instead of an earthly lamb being eaten, He becomes the unblemished sacramental Lamb that must be eaten. Now we have a New Passover: Jesus' passing over to His Father by His death and Resurrection. This fulfills the Jewish Passover and anticipates the final

Passover of the Church to God. The Mass is also about the Groom coming for His Bride, to pass her to the other side on the eighth day.[29]

The Eucharist was foreshadowed in the Old Covenant above all in the annual Passover meal celebrated every year by the Jews with unleavened bread to commemorate their hasty, liberating departure from Egypt. Jesus foretold it in His teaching, and He instituted it when He celebrated the Last Supper with His apostles in a Passover meal on Holy Thursday:

> While they were eating, he took a loaf of bread, and after blessing it he broke it, gave it to them, and said, "Take; this is my body." Then he took a cup, and after giving thanks he gave it to them, and all of them drank from it. He said to them, "This is my blood of the covenant, which is poured out for many. Truly I tell you, I will never again drink of the fruit of the vine until that day when I drink it new in the kingdom of God." (Mk 14:22-25).

Do these words sound familiar? Yes, the words of the Mass are the words of Christ. Jesus is present in the Eucharist in a true, real, and substantial way. In the Eucharist, therefore, there is present in a sacramental way — that is, under the Eucharistic species of bread and wine — Christ, God and Man, whole and entire. But how can Christ be whole and entire, yet separated as such? At Mass, consecration of bread and wine separately represents the separation of Christ's Body and Blood at Calvary. But Jesus can't die now, so His Body and Blood must remain united, and His Soul unites to both. His divinity always remains united to His humanity (His Body, Blood, and Soul) because He is God made Man. So the communicant who receives either species (the Host or the Precious Blood) receives Christ, whole and entire (all Body, Blood, Soul, and Divinity). The Mass starts with Christ being sacrificed (as a Man) and ends with Him being glorified (as God). That is why in the Eucharist we don't receive His mortal flesh, as it was in His earthly ministry (we are *not* cannibals). What we receive is His Body and Blood in His glorified humanity after He rose from the dead (He is now the Living Bread). Ultimately, we understand Jesus more in the Eucharist than we understand Him in Scripture!

The Eucharist in Scripture

As mentioned in the Introduction, chapter 6 in the Gospel of John is the most definitive proof for the existence of the Eucharist in Scripture. Without the need to reprint basically the entire chapter here, one only has to read verses 27 through 58 to get an understanding of how important this grace of God is for us mortal men. Even then, however, people did not believe (see Jn 6:60). Today, for those non-Catholics (and even 70 percent of Catholics, unfortunately) who do not believe in the Real Presence of Christ in the Eucharist, we need only cite Scripture to show that all early Christians believed in it. The term "breaking of bread" is a Eucharistic phrase in St. Luke's writings. When St. Paul was in Troas, we read, "we met to break bread" (Acts 20:7). The road to Emmaus account states that Cleopas and an unnamed disciple's "eyes were opened" and they recognized Jesus "in the breaking of the bread" (see Lk 24:30-31). Though there were no actual church buildings in the first century, Christians had already designated homes for "church" gatherings (see 1 Cor 11:18-23). And the centerpiece of the gathering — especially on Sunday, the first day of the week — was the breaking of the bread, just as it is for Catholics today. "On the first day of the week, when we met to break bread, Paul was holding a discussion with them; since he intended to leave the next day, he continued speaking until midnight." (Acts 20:7).

 Elsewhere in Scripture, it is interesting to note that the Wedding Feast at Cana (see Jn 2:1-11) foreshadowed the Precious Blood, and the multiplication of the loaves (the only miracle other than the Resurrection to appear in all four Gospels: see Mt 14:13-21; Mk 6:30-44; Lk 9:12-17; and Jn 6:1-14) foreshadowed the Eucharist. During the account, Jesus gives thanks (*says the blessing*), breaks the bread, and distributes it to His disciples. First Jesus provided the wine at Cana; now He provides the bread. Jesus gave the bread to the disciples and the disciples gave it to the crowd, just as if they were priests distributing Holy Communion today. This shows that it is God's will that heavenly food be distributed through the Church, through the consecrated hands of the priests.

Who May Receive?

Like the Sacrament of Confirmation, the Church encourages reception of First Holy Communion no earlier than the age of reason, which is 7 years old. Children are prepared to receive the Sacrament in their parish religious education programs or in Catholic schools. To receive Holy Communion one must be incorporated into the Catholic Church (baptized) and be in the state of grace — that is, not conscious of having committed grave (mortal) sin. Anyone who is conscious of having committed grave sin must first receive the Sacrament of Reconciliation before going to Communion. The Church obliges the faithful to participate at Holy Mass every Sunday and on Holy Days of Obligation, and recommends participation at Holy Mass on other days also. The Church suggests that the faithful, if they are in the state of grace, receive Holy Communion whenever they participate at Holy Mass, but it is not a requirement. Canon law states:

> After being initiated into the Most Holy Eucharist, each of the faithful is obliged to receive holy communion at least once a year. This precept must be fulfilled during the Easter season unless it is fulfilled for a just cause at another time during the year (920).

This is commonly known as the "Easter duty."

People who were married in the Church often ask me, "Can I receive Holy Communion after my divorce?" It depends. I'll go into this in more detail in the chapter on Holy Matrimony. In short, you may receive Holy Communion if you have not remarried (or have remarried after obtaining an annulment) and are in a state of grace. However, you may not receive Holy Communion if you are remarried civilly without an annulment, as the Church considers that you are still sacramentally married and therefore committing adultery. And what about non-Catholics — can they receive the Eucharist? Yes, actually, in grave necessity (such as near death) if they ask for it of their own free will, possess the required dispositions, and give evidence of holding the Catholic faith regarding the Sacrament. Of course, they would need to be baptized first if they have not already been baptized in the name of the Holy Trinity.

But more important than the "legalities" of the restrictions of receiving, focus on the *meaning* of receiving. Under the appearance of bread and wine Jesus is contained, offered, and received. Eating is always an act of reception, as is having faith, so approaching Holy Communion is an act of faith. You don't have to do anything. You only have to believe and receive.

It's Not Just a Symbol

Sadly, even Catholics often state that they believe that the Eucharist is only a symbol of the Body of Christ, not actually the Body of Christ. That is incorrect. As mentioned above, John 6 is a treasure of grace explaining the Eucharist. In that chapter Jesus says, "I am the living bread that came down from heaven. Whoever eats of this bread will live forever; and the bread that I will give for the life of the world is my flesh" (Jn 6:51). That's one of my favorite passages in the whole Bible. Jesus was speaking the truth, and we know this because He kept stressing its importance, even as the Jews disputed this issue among themselves:

> The Jews then disputed among themselves, saying, "How can this man give us his flesh to eat?" So Jesus said to them, "Very truly, I tell you, unless you eat the flesh of the Son of Man and drink his blood, you have no life in you. Those who eat my flesh and drink my blood have eternal life, and I will raise them up on the last day; for my flesh is true food and my blood is true drink. Those who eat my flesh and drink my blood abide in me, and I in them. Just as the living Father sent me, and I live because of the Father, so whoever eats me will live because of me. This is the bread that came down from heaven, not like that which your ancestors ate, and they died. But the one who eats this bread will live forever" (Jn 6:52-58).

This sixth chapter of John's Gospel, the Bread of Life discourse, is an amazing collection of statements that would be theologically problematic for a first-century Jew. The Old Testament includes numerous prohibitions against the eating of an animal's flesh with the blood, because blood was seen as the life of the being, and only God could take that life. Jesus is proposing not just eating *an animal's* flesh and blood, but *His own* flesh and blood. What's more, the Greek verb for "eat" used in Scripture here is not *phagein* (the verb normally used for human eating), but rather *trogein*, a verb that designates the way animals eat. It literally means "gnawing" or "chewing," so Jesus is talking literally here about somehow, mysteriously, eating His flesh and drinking His blood!

When reading John 6:52-58, it is common for people to ask, "Is Jesus speaking symbolically here? Or maybe He is using an expression?" Well, not likely. In Aramaic, the language that Jesus spoke, the expression "Eat the flesh, drink the blood" of someone is meant to persecute or assault them. This would certainly not be the way to earn eternal life. Therefore, many scholars have argued for a literal interpretation of Jesus' words because St. Paul says in 1 Corinthians 11:27-29 that to receive this bread unworthily brings condemnation on oneself. Thus, the bread would have to be more than symbolic. Moreover, if Jesus were speaking only symbolically, the disciples would not have walked away in John's Gospel when He said, "For my flesh is true food and my blood is true drink."

So how is this transformation (*transubstantiation*) done from bread and wine to Body and Blood? Jesus is the Word of God, and therefore His words have the power to transform a substance. Remember, *matter* is the substance and the *form* is the words. This is why the ordinary bread and wine became Christ's very Body and Blood. Now, at the consecration, the priest pronounces these words of Christ, not his own words. The priest acts, not in his own person, but *in persona Christi*, and hence he effects the transformation. This is a change of substance, a transubstantiation, and that's why we need a priest. This is incredible! It's not just symbolic. It is literal truth.

A woman approached me once and said, "You know, my family and I go to the nondenominational church down the road and we have Holy Communion."

"God bless you," I replied, "but it's not Holy Communion. It's symbolic bread and wine, or in many cases, Wonder Bread and grape juice."

Look, I'm not trying to discredit any other faith. Protestant Christians freely admit that they don't believe in transubstantiation. But we Catholics do, and the Sacrament of the Eucharist is another thing that makes us (along with the Eastern Orthodox Churches) different and unique from all other Christian churches. That's also the reason that non-Catholics are usually respectfully not invited to receive Holy Communion. Consider the word "Communion."

That means unity — a shared belief in the Real Presence of Our Lord in the Eucharist — but they don't share that same belief. The Eucharist is "the heart and summit of the Church's life," the *Catechism* states. "Since receiving this sacrament strengthens the bonds of charity between the communicant and Christ, it also reinforces the unity of the Church as the Mystical Body of Christ" (1407, 1416). It is important, therefore, to understand what the Eucharist is before receiving it. You must believe in the Sacrament to take part. We mean no disrespect to non-Catholics when we announce, usually at a wedding or funeral Mass, that only Catholics in a state of grace can receive Communion. It's not about exclusion or arrogance; it's simply about a difference in belief. Others can come up for a blessing, with arms crossed over their chest, which can be a sufficient sign of unity.

The enforcement of this rule should be a clarion call to non-Catholics — the Eucharist *is* Jesus, and He's present in every Catholic church every hour of every day around the world. Could there be a more persuasive invitation to non-Catholics? Come and learn what the Catholic faith is all about. It's miraculous! Until a person fully understands this reality *and* believes in it, receiving Communion is not proper. The issue has nothing to do with lack of inclusion; rather, it is about being properly disposed and prepared to receive. If I walk onto an airplane and announce that I want to help fly the plane, then proceed to walk up the aisle toward the cockpit, what would happen? When the pilot denies me, because I don't fully understand what I am about to do, would anybody disagree with the pilot? Or call him uncharitable or hateful? Not at all.

We also need to make absolutely sure that we are not in mortal sin when we receive the Eucharist. These days, tragically, a lot of people, including many Catholics, no longer understand the consequences of sin. Unsurprisingly, these same people do not believe in the Real Presence of Jesus in Holy Communion, or if they do, they see no problem in receiving because it may not mean much to them. That's why we had the National Eucharistic Revival, to bring back love for the Eucharist, to revive in the hearts of God's people this essential truth. We need to know who He is, be free of grave sin, and prepare ourselves.

And here's my pet peeve: perpetual tardiness of those who fail to place Mass as a priority. You want to come in and have some time for prayer, asking the Lord to prepare your heart for that intimate union you are about to experience with Him in the Eucharist. And then even after Communion, I see people heading for the exits before the final blessing — they have to be first out of the parking lot. You can't stay with Jesus just a little bit? My Marian brother, Fr. Donald Calloway, once said in a talk, "Don't forget who the first one was who left the Last Supper. It was Judas Iscariot!" That's a shocking statement, I know, but it's also a message: Don't run off! Spend time with Jesus after Communion because He wants to be with you. Spend time before the Blessed Sacrament in church or at Eucharistic Adoration. Listen to Jesus. Don't miss the grace and experiencing how much Jesus loves you and how much He wants you to consume Him. This is your chance to experience a Eucharistic revival in your own soul.

Eucharistic Miracles

A true Eucharistic miracle occurs at every Catholic Mass when the priest utters the words of consecration and the substance of the bread and wine are changed into the substance of the Body and Blood of Christ. Saint Faustina recounted several miraculous events surrounding the Eucharist. For instance:

> Once, the image was being exhibited over the altar during the Corpus Christi procession [June 20, 1935]. When the priest exposed the Blessed Sacrament, and the choir began to sing, the rays

from the image pierced the Sacred Host and spread out all over the world. Then I heard these words: **These rays of mercy will pass through you, just as they have passed through this Host, and they will go out through all the world.** At these words, profound joy invaded my soul (*Diary*, 441).

Throughout history, many people have reported miracles that brought them back to the Church. The Church has recognized more than 100 Eucharistic miracles. Many occurred during times (like ours) of weakened faith in the Real Presence. Saint Carlo Acutis designed a website on Eucharistic miracles that is still the go-to source of information.[30] And the Real Presence Association is currently translating from Italian into English reports of 120 Vatican-approved miracles. Some include bleeding hosts or the transmutation of a consecrated host into a piece of actual human cardiac (heart) muscle tissue. Did you see the Eucharistic miracle in Guadalajara, Mexico, in 2022? Scientists who analyzed the video, in which the Eucharist appears to be beating like a human heart, confirmed that the rhythm and pulsating beats mimic the exact beating of a human heart. That is now your new heart received at Mass, if you are open to receive it!

One of the earliest documented Eucharistic miracles was recorded by the Desert Fathers in Egypt, who were among the first Christian monks. One monk had doubts about the Real Presence of Jesus in the consecrated bread and wine, and his two brother monks prayed for his faith. As the three of them celebrated Mass, instead of the bread they placed on the altar, they saw a small child. An angel appeared and cut the Child into small pieces, pouring His Blood into the chalice. When it came time to receive Holy Communion, the skeptical monk alone received a morsel of bloody flesh. He cried out, "Lord, I believe that this bread is your flesh and this chalice your blood!" Immediately the flesh regained the appearance of bread! The other two monks gained a new appreciation of transubstantiation, and stated, "God knows human nature and that man cannot eat raw flesh, and that is why He has changed His Body into bread and His Blood into wine for those who receive it in faith."[31] Again, *Wow!*

But please understand that consuming the Eucharist is *not* cannibalism. Catholics have been accused of that since the early days of the Church. In fact, St. Justin Martyr refuted claims of "eating human flesh" in his *First Apology*, written between A.D. 153 and 155:

> For not as common bread and common drink do we receive these; but in like manner as Jesus Christ our Savior, having been made flesh by the Word of God, had both flesh and blood for our salvation, so likewise have we been taught that the food which is blessed by the prayer of His word, and from which our blood and flesh by transmutation are nourished, is the flesh and blood of that Jesus who was made flesh.[32]

As we mentioned earlier, we are consuming the *glorified* Body and Blood of Christ, not the blood-and-flesh tissue in His human form that we would have seen when He was walking the earth. The Eucharist, as the glorified Body and Blood of Jesus, is very much alive in a sacramental manner, under the Eucharistic species of bread and wine. In reality, we are uniting our bodies within Holy Communion with the risen and glorified Body and Blood of Jesus. So while the substance of the bread and wine has changed to Christ's Body and Blood, the accidents (the appearance) of bread and wine still exist. For instance, the molecular structure of bread would appear intact under a microscope. That is the miracle.

Speaking of miracles, in all Eucharistic miracles the blood tested is consistently found to be AB blood (specifically AB+), similar to the Host of Lanciano and the blood found on the Holy Shroud of Turin.[33] This AB blood is the universal *receiver* rather than universal donor, however. This is surprising because we often think of Jesus being the ultimate *donor* of His Blood, not receiving blood. So why would Jesus' Blood be globally receptive instead of a universal donor? A universal receiver means they can take any blood type and make it their own (all can be received). We generally speak of "receiving" Christ in Holy Communion. This means we take it into us and make it part of us. But actually something greater happens. We become a part of Him! When we receive Holy Communion, "it's less about Christ becoming part of us than it is we becoming ever more part of Him, and, by extension, more part of His Body, the Church. 'Really partaking of the body of the Lord in the breaking of the Eucharistic bread,' the Council Fathers teach us, 'we are taken up into communion with Him and with one another.'"[34] Saint Irenaeus said, "our communicated flesh is not only nourished by Christ's Body and Blood, but is also 'in fact a member of Him.'"[35] With the Blood of a universal recipient, Christ is capable of receiving our stained blood. He took on the sins of the world so that no sinner is excluded from being taken up into His divine life.

Regarding the blood of these bleeding Hosts, the fact that the outer part of the blood on the Host has been coagulated for years, while the inner part of the blood continues to remain fresh, indicates that the tissue continues to effuse fresh blood, which is unexplainable. Furthermore, the blood contains proteins indicating elevated metabolism in the person from which the tissue came, like that found during trauma. The blood has white blood cells, so the tissue is still living (or was removed from the body while it was alive) and the blood has hemoglobin and DNA of human origin. These startling characteristics have been proven consistent across numerous tests done on bleeding hosts.[36]

Most all tests of approved Eucharistic miracles (such as bleeding Hosts) have provided a fascinating fact: When the Host was examined, it was revealed that the tissue found corresponds to the muscle of the human heart (myocardium). This connects to the traditional prayer, "Jesus, make my heart like unto Thine." In fact, we can now see how it is literally true. When the priest says at Mass, "Lift up your hearts," and you respond, "We lift them up to the Lord," the Lord is preparing you to receive a heart transplant. You are basically saying, "Lord, I give you my stony heart, because my heart is broken and hardened," and then He gives you His Heart — literally! He is replacing your stone-cold heart with His Heart, full of mercy and love.

Our Catholic faith, of course, should not be based on miracles alone. But the many reports of Eucharistic miracles have strengthened the faith of many and reminded them of the miracle that takes place at every Catholic Mass. That's amazing grace!

The Meaning of the Mass

As we said, a true Eucharistic miracle happens at every Mass. But is the Mass in the Bible? What about in the Book of Revelation? Isn't this book about the Antichrist and the Rapture? No. Neither of these terms is mentioned in the entire book! As Dr. Scott Hahn points out in his life-changing volume *The Lamb's Supper*, the Book of Revelation is all about the Catholic Mass and the Eucharist.[37] The priesthood (20:6); celibacy (14:4); the High Priest, robes, and candles (1:13); an altar, censer, rising incense, prayers of the saints (8:3-4); and the Eucharist (2:17) are all in the description of the events of Revelation. Even the words that are frequent in the Catholic Mass are found in this book, such as *Holy, Holy, Holy* (4:8), *Alleluia* (19:1), and the *Gloria* (15:3). We have the Penitential Rite, where we are called to repent; the Lamb of God (mentioned 28 times); altars, books, and chalices. There are white robes, saints, and the sacrifice of the Lamb, which has to be eaten or the sacrifice is invalid. It is all there! Scott Hahn says the Mass is on every page; it is truly Heaven on earth.

Hahn points out that chapters 1 to 11 are similar to the Liturgy of the Word at Mass, because the High Priest emerges at the altar and goes to the book to reveal its contents. Chapters 13 to 22 are similar to the Liturgy of the Eucharist because the people are fed manna from Heaven (2:17), and the wine in the chalices is turned into blood! Yes, just like the two parts of the Mass: We hear about Jesus (Liturgy of the Word) and then we meet Jesus (the Liturgy of the Eucharist). So, Christ is present in Heaven and on Earth at the Mass. Hahn adds, if you make it to Mass, you've made it to Heaven.[38] The Church is in Heaven and the Kingdom is on earth, so the Mass links the two. Heavenly glory is unveiled in the earthly Liturgy; in fact, the Greek word *apocalypse* means "unveiling," not "complete destruction." Let us remember to contemplate these awesome connections the next time we attend Mass.

Finally, regarding the Eucharist, we often think of Jesus, as we should, but what about the other members of the Trinity? Are They part of Holy Communion? We know that Divine Mercy is the perfect love of the Trinity overflowing outside of itself to us, which started with Creation. But God didn't stop there. After mankind sinned and "got broken," God sent His Son to redeem us in the second great act of Mercy. And while the Second Person of the Trinity is the only One to become Incarnate, and thus the only One present sacramentally in the Eucharist, the Trinity is present as well. Saint Faustina said, "Once after Holy Communion, I heard these words: **You are Our dwelling place.** At that moment, I felt in my soul the presence of the Holy Trinity, the Father, the Son, and the Holy Spirit" (*Diary*, 451).

Holy Communion is the divine activity of love eternally taking place within the Trinity, not just Jesus. Yes, only Christ is present sacramentally in the Eucharist as we said, under the appearance of bread and wine, but the Father and the Holy Spirit are also present with Christ because of the perfect unity of the Trinity. The Father and the Holy Spirit are consubstantial with Christ (having the same nature), so by what we call *circumincession*, each of the three Persons is eternally present in each other, while still remaining distinct. Moreover, St. Thérèse of Lisieux realized that not only was the Trinity about to dwell in her, but since the angels and saints in Heaven are "perfectly incorporated into Christ," all of Heaven would come to dwell in her as well. She said, "Heaven itself dwelt in my soul, in receiving a visit from Our Divine Lord."[39] When we receive Christ sacramentally, through *concomitance* the Father and the Holy Spirit become present with Christ — not sacramentally, but nonetheless in a true and substantial way. Wow, the Eucharist is even more than I bet you knew it was!

Why did Jesus call Himself the Bread of Life in the Gospel of John? It also ties to the Trinity, specifically the Father, and we can see connections with God's Word given to Israel across its history. The idea of the Torah (the Word of God) as bread was common in Jewish thinking. We aren't to just "live on bread alone but by every word that comes from the mouth of the LORD" (Dt 8:3). Who came from the mouth of God the Father? Jesus (the Word), so we are to live on Him, and we do so in the Eucharist. Jews understood that God promised them manna from Heaven to sustain them on their journey (see Ex 16). Bread is the very staple of life. We could not live without food for very long. That's why we have the Mass! *Mass* comes from the Latin word *missa*, "dismissal," which implies a "mission." Be fed and go!

THE SACRAMENTS OF HEALING

Reconciliation
(Penance or Confession)

> Those who approach the sacrament of Penance obtain pardon from God's mercy for the offense committed against him, and are, at the same time, reconciled with the Church which they have wounded by their sins and which by charity, by example, and by prayer labors for their conversion.
>
> — *Catechism of the Catholic Church*, 1422

The Sacrament of Reconciliation, also called Penance (or simply Confession), is not a human invention. Once we sin, we must not seek pardon on our own terms, but on God's terms, as we will explain. This is why He gave us Confession.

Saint Faustina holds the key for us in her *Diary*. Jesus told St. Faustina that God's mercy primarily flows to us first in Scripture, but then in Reconciliation, the Sacrament of forgiveness and mercy:

> **Encourage souls to place great trust in My fathomless mercy. Let the weak, sinful soul have no fear to approach Me, for even if it had more sins than there are grains of sand in the world, all would be drowned in the unmeasurable depths of My mercy** (*Diary*, 1059).

The third way God's mercy flows to us is the Eucharist, which Jesus says is love greater than death. In the Image of Divine

Mercy, the rays coming from our Lord's Sacred Heart represent the Precious Blood of Holy Communion (the red ray) and the cleansing waters of Confession and Baptism (the pale ray). Satan's only two tools, sin and death, are wiped out by these two rays found in the Image of Divine Mercy (shown on this book's inside front cover). Why?

Here we can ask the simple question: What wipes away sin? Answer: The cleansing waters of Baptism and Confession (the pale ray). The Church Fathers taught that the water that flowed from the side of Christ represents Baptism, which comprehensively forgives sins — and sacramental Confession is an extension and renewal of baptismal grace: "a second plank of salvation" to cling to after we have made a shipwreck of our faith and baptismal vocation by committing mortal sin. That is why Jesus said, **"When you go to confession, to this fountain of My mercy, the Blood and Water which came forth from My Heart always flows down upon your soul and ennobles it. Every time you go to confession, immerse yourself entirely in My mercy, with great trust, so that I may pour the bounty of My grace upon your soul"** (*Diary*, 1602). Saint Faustina wrote, "O God, You are compassion itself for the greatest sinners who sincerely repent. The greater the sinner, the greater his right to God's mercy" (*Diary*, 423).

With his thousands of hours in the confessional, St. Pio of Pietrelcina (Padre Pio) taught the value of regular Confession. He urged all believers to confess at least once a week. "Even if a room is closed," he said, "it is necessary to dust it after a week." He added, "God runs after the most stubborn souls. They cost him too much to abandon them."[40] Add to that the persistence of our Blessed Mother, who over the past 200 years has been calling mankind to penance and conversion. This was the essence of her messages, especially in her apparitions at Lourdes and Fatima. At Fatima and Akita, she expressed the seriousness of this call in relation to an impending chastisement that will come upon the world if mankind doesn't repent and turn back to God. Could there be a better reason to return to the Sacrament of Confession?

Note: Regarding Satan's second tool, death, what conquers that? Answer: Life. And what was life to the Jews? Blood, because blood gives life to any being. No human can live without blood. Thus we have the second ray, the red ray, which is the Precious Blood (the Eucharist) conquering death so that we may have eternal life.

Form, Matter, Minister

In Matthew 16:19 and 18:18, and in John 20:23, Christ entrusted the ministry of Reconciliation to His apostles. We can extend that to the bishops, who are their successors, and to the priests, who are the collaborators of the bishops, as the *ministers* of the Sacrament. It is fitting that God would want His mercy to continue, even after the apostles were martyred, allowing the priests to become instruments of God's mercy and justice. Priests exercise their power of forgiving sins using the words "I absolve you of your sins, in the name of the Father, and of the Son, and of the Holy Spirit." Without any exception, and under very severe penalties, they must maintain "the sacramental seal," which means absolute secrecy about the sins revealed during Confession.

By its very name, Reconciliation means we are reconciled back to God, Whom we have offended through our sins. The Sacrament absolves our sins and puts us back on the path toward Heaven. This is the "state of grace" required to receive Holy Communion worthily. Recall the forceful words of St. Paul to the early Christians, which still ring true today:

> So whoever is in Christ is a new creation: the old things have passed away; behold, new things have come. And all this is from God, who has reconciled us to himself through Christ and given us the ministry of reconciliation, namely, God

was reconciling the world to himself in Christ, not counting their trespasses against them and entrusting to us the message of reconciliation. So we are ambassadors for Christ, as if God were appealing through us. We implore you on behalf of Christ, be reconciled to God. For our sake he made him to be sin who did not know sin, so that we might become the righteousness of God in him (2 Cor 5:17-21).[41]

Before you go to Confession, make a good *Examination of Conscience* (I suggest how a little later). Try to be thorough, but don't be terrified of forgetting a sin. Ask the Holy Spirit to remind you of anything you're forgetting. Remember that grave or mortal sins *must* be confessed, while venial sins *may* be confessed, especially if they have become habitual or there are a great many. The *matter* of Reconciliation is the act of confessing one's sins, including contrition and sorrow for them, while the *form* is the priest's words of absolution, typically, "I absolve you from your sins in the name of the Father, and of the Son, and of the Holy Spirit." Confessions may be held in confessionals in churches; in pews or on chairs in the church; outside; or wherever some measure of privacy is possible. Often, you will have the choice to either confess to the priest face-to-face or from behind a screen. If both options are available, it is your choice which to use, but surprisingly, "behind the screen" is the more traditional way.

What is Sin?

In order for a person to understand their need for Confession, it is imperative that they first understand what sin is, and therefore their need for forgiveness. Sin is introducing disharmony into God's otherwise perfect universe. When we sin, we turn away from God, even if our action is not aimed directly at Him. For centuries, the Catholic Church provided a moral compass to the world, and people followed it. But today the world is not open to this corrective action from God's Church. The world believes the Church should be silenced so that "anything goes" and people can sin in peace.

Recall the story of Herod and John the Baptist. "Herod the ruler, who had been reproved by him [John] for Herodias, his brother's wife, and because of all the evil things that Herod had done, added to them all by shutting up John in prison" (Lk 3:19-20). Herodias insisted that Herod later kill the Baptist because she didn't want to be reminded of their sin — they wanted to continue to "sin in peace," so to speak. It seems the same is true of the world today, with the world basically saying to the Church, "I don't want you convicting me of sin, so I have to eliminate you." Yes, the Church lovingly convicts us of sin, but it does this not to be judgmental or hateful, but because it wants you to get to Heaven. To condone sin is a death sentence of the soul, so if we really love a person, we don't want that for them. "Admonishing the Sinner" is actually one of the Corporal Works of Mercy!

To explain it further, sin is any word, deed, or desire contrary to the eternal law; basically, it is turning away from the Creator and fixing your gaze on the creature, the created thing, or worst of all yourself. Sin is the opposite of charity (which is needed for salvation) and removes God's grace from your soul. Jesus told St. Faustina, **"Know without doubt, and once and for all, that only mortal sin drives Me out of a soul, and nothing else"** (*Diary*, 1181). Yes, left to ourselves we can't overcome these things, but with God's grace in the Sacraments, we can.

I remember hearing a priest say, "People seem to think there's nothing wrong as long as they're not killing anybody. 'I don't have to worry,' they say. 'I'm going to Heaven because I'm a good person. I've never killed anybody.' Yeah, you're a good person if the only person you're comparing yourself to is Hitler." You don't have to just avoid murder to realize you're in need of God's mercy. We are all really in need of God's mercy because the saints have warned us that slipping into hell may be easier than you think.

However, they all give us the remedy to avoid that: humility. Saint Francis de Sales wrote, "Hell is full of good intentions and wills" (a variation of Sir 21:10: "The way of sinners is smoothly paved with stones, but at its end is the pit of Hades"). Basically, St. Francis means there are people in hell who worked at a soup kitchen. There are people in hell who donated to their church. There are even people in hell who sat in the first pew at Sunday Mass. But he said there's not one soul in hell with the virtue of humility. Likewise, he said there are many souls in Heaven who had many, many vices (they have now been purified). There are souls in Heaven who have looked at pornography, or were hooked on drugs and alcohol. But there's not one soul in Heaven with the vice of pride. By planning to go to Confession, we are cooperating with God's grace and are demonstrating to Him that we are growing in the virtue of humility.

How to Prepare for a Good Confession

Before going to Confession, perform an Examination of Conscience, which is a mental exercise to reflect on your thoughts, words, and deeds since your last Confession that are contrary to the will of God. There are two types of sins: venial and mortal. The difference between them is a matter of degree, gravity, and intention. A venial sin, according to the *Catechism*, "does not deprive the sinner of sanctifying grace, friendship with God, charity, and consequently eternal happiness" (1863). Gossip, for instance, is a venial sin if it is done occasionally and without any evil intention. However, if your gossip habit becomes incessant and deliberate, with the intention of harming someone's reputation, it is an objectively grave matter (serious sin) that may be mortal.

Mortal sin, the *Catechism* explains, "results in the loss of charity and the privation of sanctifying grace, that is, of the state of grace" (1861). Please don't be confused into believing "sin is sin" and there are no degrees, as some people claim. Saint John explains that some sin is mortal (deadly) and some sin is not (see 1 Jn 5:16-17). Thus, the Church has always taught the danger of the latter: "To die in mortal [deadly] sin without repenting and accepting God's merciful love means remaining separated from him forever by our own free choice."[42] That's why God's mercy in Confession is so important; it repairs our relationship with God and the world by forgiving those deadly (mortal) sins.

Three conditions must be present for a sin to be mortal: It must be a grave matter, you must know it's a sin, and you must freely choose it (meaning you had free will at the time of the sin). In other words, your conscience knows it is wrong, yet you still freely choose to commit the sin. So, lying on the couch, perfectly healthy, on Sunday morning and saying, "I just don't want to be bothered with going to church today," is a mortal sin. Most Catholics don't know sins such as missing Mass without reason, or other common sins such as masturbation, criticizing/denying official Church dogma (such as Mary's Assumption), or lack of forgiveness even when we have done nothing wrong to the person who hurt us, are examples of grave sins that are mortal if committed with knowledge and free will.

Keep in mind, however, that not all sins that are grave matter are necessarily mortal. I remember praying at an abortion clinic years ago and the people on the sidewalk were shouting at the young women entering the facility, angrily announcing that they were committing mortal sin. In one sense, the intent of the protesters was good since they were trying to stop the women from the sin of abortion, which is objectively grave matter. However, the premature judgment may be problematic because the sin of abortion in this case, shockingly, may not be mortal. It depends again on knowledge and free will.

I remember how moved I was when one of the women who was entering the clinic suddenly turned to the protesters and shouted in return, "Do you think I want this abortion? I don't! But my boyfriend said if I don't do this, he will kill me and the baby — and trust me, he will do it!" A woman behind me loudly exclaimed, "Well, just leave him!" To which the woman replied, "Do you think it is that easy? You have NO idea what my life is like!" Wow, I was greatly impacted by her words and prayed for her as she went into the clinic.

So back to the point at hand: Would this abortion be a mortal sin? While it is certainly an objectively grave sin, it may not be mortal since she was not freely choosing to commit the sin. She didn't want to take the life of the baby and she didn't appear to have free will; thus, only God can judge the true condition of her soul. So let's be careful before we proclaim that any particular person is in a state of mortal sin.

Now, if it's been awhile since your last Confession, I recommend going through the Ten Commandments and the Seven Deadly Sins to identify your venial and mortal sins against God and neighbor, to help you make a good and thorough Confession. Let's look first at the Ten Commandments:

1. *I am the Lord your God; you shall not have other gods before Me.* Do I love with all my heart the Lord who loves me? Do I pray daily and trust in Him, or have I failed to place Him first in my heart and instead value the things of the world more, such as money, sex, and power? Have I placed myself on the throne of my heart, putting my will ahead of God's will and in essence loving myself more than God?

2. ***You shall not take the name of the Lord your God in vain.*** Do I revere God's name, or have I taken it lightly, carelessly (OMG!), or blasphemously, even wishing evil on others? Do I realize that using God's name in vain to damn someone is actually having that very same negative effect on my soul if I don't repent of it? Have I received Jesus worthily in Holy Communion? If not, I am receiving Him in vain.

3. ***Remember to keep holy the Lord's Day.*** Do I worship the Lord by taking part in Mass on Sundays and Holy Days of Obligation, or have I been indifferent to the Eucharist, to Christ's redeeming love, preferring earthly goods? Is Sunday my day of rest and prayer, or have I placed work to gain success for myself as my priority? Have I caused others to not have time for the Lord on this day by shopping and doing unnecessary errands, activities, and so on?

4. ***Honor your father and your mother.*** Have I loved and respected my parents? Have I obeyed them in terms of all they have reasonably asked of me? Do I come to their aid when they're in need or in their elderly years? Do I seek to maintain good communication with them? Have I caused conflict in my family? Do I neglect my duties to my own spouse or children? Do I provide a good example as a parent on how to live the Catholic faith? Do I obey just civil laws and authority, even on small things like speed limits while driving?

5. ***You shall not kill.*** Have I loved my neighbor, or have I physically harmed or hastened the death of another through violence, abortion, euthanasia, drugs, or abuse? Has my lifestyle

been harmful to my family and self, spiritually and physically? Do I eat or drink immoderately, thus damaging my body, the temple of the Holy Spirit? Have I aided in destroying (thus killing) someone's reputation through gossip or slander?

6. and 9. *You shall not commit adultery; you shall not covet your neighbor's wife.* Have I been impure in thoughts, words, and actions, or have I been unfaithful to my spouse or desirous of another? Have I been sexually active outside of marriage, or with another of the same sex? Have I indulged in pornography, masturbation, contraception, and other sexual sins? Have I led others into sexual sin? Have I voluntarily imagined being with someone other than my spouse during the marital act? Do I freely and willingly fantasize about others in an impure and improper way, thus committing adultery in my heart?

7. and 10. *You shall not steal; you shall not covet your neighbor's goods.* Do I respect another's goods, or have I been envious and greedy, even taking what belongs to another? Have I paid my debts? Have I wasted time at home, school, or work, stealing from my employer on my time card? Have I squandered my resources on non-essentials? Have I failed to work for justice or to support the poor and the Church? Am I always unhappy with what God gave me and been desirous of what others have? Do I believe that the measure of people's worth, including my own, is based on their material holdings?

8. *You shall not bear false witness against your neighbor.* Have I been honest, or have I lied, gossiped, given false testimony, ruined the good name of another, broken confidentiality, or denied the truth out of pride or hypocrisy? Have I shown mercy to others? Am I ashamed to confess a mortal sin? Have I caused division between others by stating things that are not true (calumny) to others or by stating things to others that are true, but to people who have no right to know such information (detraction)?[43]

Another good way to identify your sins is to reflect on the Seven Deadly Sins:

Pride. The proud person thinks he or she is above everyone else. The Book of Proverbs notes, "Pride goes before destruction, and a haughty spirit before a fall" (Prov 16:18).

Envy. When we are envious, we are actually condemning God, thinking He did a bad job with the gifts and goods of His creation. The envious person is not content with what God gave him in life and only wants what God gave to others, seeking to even destroy that other person to gain what they have.

Wrath. Admit it: Anger can be seductive and satisfying. But it is also destructive and wrong. If we are not in a state of grace, it's easier to lash out than to show mercy.

Sloth. Who hasn't experienced bouts of laziness and put off until tomorrow what can easily be done today? Saint Thomas Aquinas defined sloth as an aimless "tendency to wander." And this is not just laziness in a physical sense — we may be very lazy spiritually by failing to pray, meditate, etc.

Avarice. Here's a fancy word for greed. Consumerism is rampant and seductive: Do you really need that extra pair of sneakers or the latest version of a cellphone, or could your money be better used to help others in need?

Gluttony. It's not just about overeating. It's about placing too much emphasis on things, whether food or consumer goods. Too much internet, television, comfort, etc.

Lust. Pope St. John Paul II reportedly said, "Chastity is the work of a lifetime." Avoiding lust and mastering our emotions and passions in a culture opposed to sexual morality is a challenge, but with God all things are possible.

These sins may be venial or mortal, depending on the circumstances. We mentioned that although it is not a requirement to confess venial sins, confessing these common sins is recommended by the Church because:

- It helps us to form a correct conscience.
- It helps us fight against evil tendencies. (Grace helps us to develop proper behavior or *habitus*.)
- It allows us to be healed by Christ.
- It helps us progress in the life of the Spirit through the humility inspired by seeing our sheer amount of sin.

How to Make a Good Confession

Once we know our sins through a thorough Examination of Conscience, it is now time to go to the Sacrament of Reconciliation. When going into the confessional or sitting down opposite a priest, some people aren't sure what to do. That's okay — the priest will walk you through it. Begin with, "Bless me, Father, for I have sinned. My last Confession was. ..." If you cannot remember when your last Confession was, just be honest and give an estimate. Don't be embarrassed. Remember that, according to Canon law, "After having reached the age of discretion, each member of the faithful is obliged to confess faithfully his or her grave sins at least once a year" (989). So if you haven't been to Confession in over a year, the first thing you want to confess is not having been to Confession in over a year. The priest is glad you have come to Confession — he's not going to judge you for how long a time (or how short!) it's been since your last Confession.

Confess your sins in number (the times committed) and in kind (what the sin was, without graphic details) to the best of your recollection. If you cannot remember, give an estimate, or indicate when something was committed more than once. So if you've committed a sin like, say, swearing, try your best to remember how many times you've done it, and what kind of swearing it was. Did you swear out loud at someone or was it an internal blurt? Did you condemn them directly, or was it said in general, not directed at anybody specific? Did you use the Lord's name in vain? That is very serious as you could actually be placing a curse on someone when you do it.

Now let's suppose it's a sexual sin. You do not need to explain things in detail. However, when you say, "Father, I was impure," for example, the priest may ask you if this was with yourself or with another person. And was it just thoughts, or was it actions? Was it homosexual or heterosexual? Are you married? Because if so, now you have committed adultery against your spouse. After confessing at least all grave sins you can remember, conclude with, "For these sins and all others I have forgotten or did not discern, I am truly sorry." The priest will give you a penance (prayers to recite, for example) and ask you to pray an Act of Contrition. While many know the traditional version — "O my God, I am heartily sorry for having offended thee ... " — the Church actually recommends another version, which is very powerful and easy to remember. It's called the Jesus Prayer: "Lord Jesus Christ, Son of the living God, have mercy on me, a poor sinner. Amen."

The priest will then say the words of absolution. You have been absolved so long as a validly-ordained priest prays at least these words over you: "I absolve you from your sins, in the name of the Father, and of the Son, and of the Holy Spirit." Trust in Jesus, because your sins have truly been forgiven and washed away. Sometimes the priest does not ask you to say the Act of Contrition, and that's okay — just say it as soon as you leave the confessional.

What about general absolution? When I was young, my mom used to take me to the diocese of Toledo, Ohio, where we would go to what was called General Penance. We would go into the church and stand there, and the priest would say, "Okay, now think of your sins and I'm going to give you general absolution." The problem is, this is not allowed by the Church, except in extraordinary circumstances, such as a mid-air emergency or time of war, when the priest forgives many people at once without hearing individual Confessions. Please keep in mind this is different from the acceptable practice of a "communal penance service" that you may see advertised in your bulletin during Advent or Lent. This is when many people gather at a church, prayers of preparation are said, and then several priests spread out to hear Confessions. This is acceptable; the key is that you are still having your Confession heard individually by one priest, not just recalling our sins in your mind with the priest absolving everyone of their sins at one time.

Where is Confession in the Bible?

Christ's delegation of the power to forgive sins is in Scripture. Jesus told St. Peter, "I will give you the keys of the kingdom of heaven, and whatever you bind on earth will be bound in heaven, and whatever you loose on earth will be loosed in heaven" (Mt 16:19; also Mt 18:18). Jesus had the ultimate authority to forgive sins on earth, and if you have ultimate authority, you have the power to delegate that authority. And Jesus did delegate to the ministers of His Church. On the eighth day after the Resurrection (when today we celebrate, appropriately, Divine Mercy Sunday), the Risen Lord came to the apostles in the Upper Room:

> Jesus said to them again, "Peace be with you. As the Father has sent me, so I send you." When he had said this, he breathed on them and said to them, "Receive the Holy Spirit. If you forgive the sins of any, they are forgiven them; if you retain the sins of any, they are retained" (Jn 20:21-23).

Here Jesus "breathed" on His disciples and gave them the Holy Spirit. It was analogous to when God breathed life into Adam, but He now breathes "new life" into His people. The apostles were then given the authority to forgive sin in Christ's Name (the grace of forgiveness comes from Jesus, but it goes through the priest). And with this full authority, they now had the power to delegate that authority, which is what we call Apostolic Succession. From St. Peter on down 2,000 years to the present, there is an unbroken line of ordained priests, all given the power of the Holy Spirit to forgive sins. "Peter forgives sins, and welcomes penitents with complete joy, and firmly maintains that this power has been granted by God to all priests," wrote St.

Peter Chrysologus, Doctor of the Church. "For after his denial Peter would have lost the glory of being an apostle as well as life, if he had not had a fresh start through penitence. And if Peter returned by means of penitence, who can survive without penitence?"[44]

In his epistle, St. James addressed the first Christians and reinforced the authority of the priest to forgive sins:

> Is anyone among you sick? He should summon the presbyters of the church, and they should pray over him and anoint [him] with oil in the name of the Lord, and the prayer of faith will save the sick person, and the Lord will raise him up. If he has committed any sins, he will be forgiven. Therefore, confess your sins to one another and pray for one another, that you may be healed. The fervent prayer of a righteous person is very powerful (Jas 5:14-16).[45]

Notice also the words in James that sins are forgiven by the priests in the Sacrament of the Sick (Anointing). This is another example of man's granted authority to forgive sins on earth. When James says, "Therefore, confess your sins to one another," since he mentioned nobody else, he is still talking about the priests. This is yet another reason we have Confession.

Let's also recall the passage about Jesus healing the leper (see Mt 8:1-4). The Jews viewed leprosy as something analogous to mortal sin. It deteriorated and disfigured people, symbolic of what sin does to the soul. The Jews believed that leprosy of the body was an outward manifestation of the person's sins. It rendered someone unclean and therefore incapable of engaging in the act of worship. It is not accidental that the person in ancient Israel who examined the patient after a hopeful cure was the priest (see Lev 14:2-9). The priest's job was to monitor the whole process of Israelite worship, including who could and couldn't participate in the Temple. So after Jesus healed the leper, did He dismiss him and send him home? No, His command was for the man to go to the priest to be declared clean, in keeping with Jewish custom. In Leviticus, it was the priest who declared them clean, so then they could re-engage in public worship. It is the same for us today: Jesus forgives us and heals us, but it is the priest in the confessional who announces the words of absolution and declares you clean. That way, you know you have been guaranteed forgiveness.

Confess to a Man? *In Persona Christi*

This Church requirement of the Sacrament of Reconciliation is often met with resistance. Often Catholics will say, "I don't confess my sins to a man; I confess directly to God!" While at first this sounds logical, God set up our sacramental system to include Confession to His priests because we need a spiritual guide even to know that some things are sins. If you "confess on your own," how is that effective when one person thinks missing Mass, for example, is a sin, yet another person does not? God gave priests to help you know such things. Catholics confess their sins to God *and* to God's ministers as directed, not just to God.

Protestants deny that Christ gave His disciples the power to forgive sins (see Jn 20:23), but God breathed on the priests (the only other time God breathed on man was at creation), so this is life-giving power, a new creation, that has now been passed down through Apostolic Succession to the priests of today. Some Protestants believe their pastors wash away sins in Baptism, so why can't priests do the same in Confession? Protestants believe that God uses their ministers to provide physical healing, so why can't God use priests for spiritual healing? Confession is not a human invention; we must not seek pardon on our own terms but on God's terms. We can't just go to our room or look to the sky, announce our sins, and have them forgiven, because Christ didn't give that authority to our room or to the sky.

When people ask, "Why can't I just ask God directly to forgive my sins?" well, you can, but the grace of forgiveness comes from God on His terms, and He set it up to go through the priest. Christ forgave sins on Earth to show He had ultimate authority to do so. As I mentioned, when you have ultimate authority, you have the power to delegate that authority. When I ran my own business in North Carolina prior to becoming a Marian priest, I had ultimate authority in business affairs because I created the company (like Christ created the Church). But when I would leave on a business trip, I would say to my manager, "While I'm gone, you're in charge. If there is a bill to pay, you pay it. If there is someone to fire, you fire. If there is someone to hire, you hire." They acted in my name, in the person of me. Well, that's the role of the priest in the Church that Christ established. Christ established the priesthood to be *in persona Christi*, in the Person of Christ. Jesus forgave sins and He still does, but He gave that power to His representatives on Earth to act in His name. If we are asking God for forgiveness, we cannot have the pride to do it "our way" rather than the way He designed for us.

When Jesus said, "Whose sins you forgive are forgiven in Heaven, and whose sins you retain are retained in Heaven," He is basically explaining that Heaven has to follow the priest. If the priest says you are forgiven, you are forgiven in Heaven. If Confession is not needed, Christ's grant of this power to forgive would be insignificant! Jesus gave authority to forgive and *not to forgive* — so the priest needs to hear sins to make that determination. Then, when you go to the confessional and the priest raises his right hand and he says, "Through the ministry of the Church, may God give you pardon and peace. And I absolve you from your sins, in the Name of the Father, and the Son, and the Holy Spirit, Amen," there's no wondering, *Am I forgiven?* or *I hope I am forgiven.* You are guaranteed forgiveness or Jesus is a liar, and nobody will claim that.

Saint Faustina gave an excellent testimony to the power the priest has to forgive sins. She said, "Once, when a certain doubt rose within me shortly before Holy Communion, the Seraph with the Lord Jesus stood before me again. I asked the Lord Jesus, and not receiving an answer, I said to the Seraph, 'Could you perhaps hear my confession?' And he answered me, 'No spirit in heaven has that power.' And at that moment, the Sacred Host rested on my lips" (*Diary*, 1677). Wow! Nobody other than a priest was given that power by God.

The grace of forgiveness doesn't *come* from the priest, but from God, and goes *through* the priest. Only God has the ultimate authority to forgive sins, but that means, as we said, He has the power to delegate that authority, and He did. He uses the priest as His tool, His representative. Jesus told St. Faustina, **"When you approach the confessional, know this, that I Myself am waiting there for you. I am only hidden by the priest, but I Myself act in your soul"** (*Diary*, 1602). He also said, **"Tell souls where they are to look for solace, that is, in the Tribunal of Mercy [the Sacrament of Reconciliation]. There the greatest miracles take place [and] are incessantly repeated"** (*Diary*, 1448). It is also interesting to note that St. Faustina wrote that going to Confession is more than just asking for and receiving forgiveness. She said it's where we come to be healed and educated as well. "We come to be educated — like a small child, our soul has constant need of education," she wrote. "A soul which sincerely wants to advance in perfection must observe strictly the advice given by the spiritual director. There is as much holiness as there is dependence" (*Diary*, 377).

Doctor of the Soul

Nobody disputes that we need to take our bodily ailments to the doctor of the body. Medical doctors counsel us on what to do, what medicine to take, and how to find healing in our life. Why, then, should we not take our ailing spirit to the "doctor of the soul," the priest, for healing as well? When I was growing up in Holly, Michigan, we had a young, handsome priest at St. Rita Parish. I remember my mom and some of the neighborhood ladies would talk about this priest. One of the ladies said, "I'm not going to *that* priest. He's too young. And he's not holy enough because I see the way he looks at those young ladies!" They all agreed. Yet those same ladies and my mom all went to the same doctor in town. He reeked of alcohol, was 30 pounds overweight, and smoked like a chimney. He was anything *but* healthy! And yet my mom took me to this guy to get me healthy. I remember my mom would say, "It's not about who the doctor is, it's about what he can do for you. He knows how to heal you." Well, then, the same could be said about the priest. No matter how broken the priest is, no matter how much of an unappealing guy you think he might be, he can help you in that confessional because he was given that power as a priest. He is a doctor of the soul, ready to offer counsel and encouragement, and most importantly the healing grace of absolution. It helps to know that the efficacy of the Sacraments does not depend upon the personal holiness of the priest; however, the fruits of the Sacraments do depend on the dispositions of the one who receives the Sacraments.

I also remember my mom saying, "Oh, well, that priest can't counsel me in Confession because priests have never been married. They've never had a family. How is he going to help me with marriage problems?" Well, all priests come from families, some from very dysfunctional families, so they have some very practical insight. Let's go back to the example of the doctor. How many of you have been cured by a doctor? Did you ever ask, "Doctor, I want to know if you have ever had cancer, because if you haven't had cancer, then I don't think you're going to know how to treat me for cancer." I'm not aware of any logical person who would make that statement. Regardless of whether the priest has ever been married or not — some have been earlier in their lives, and have been widowed or had their marriage annulled — it doesn't mean he can't help you. He can help because he understands what the Church teaches about marriage and what you need to do to keep your marriage holy. He was trained in seminary to explain how you can live your life according to the moral laws of the Church. Not rules so much, but road maps to get you and your spouse to Heaven.

If you are frustrated by your priest, take the advice of St. Faustina. She urges us to pray for the priest before we approach the confessional, "that he might obtain the light of the Holy Spirit" and better understand you and your concerns, and that God will give him the grace and wisdom to know how to guide you (see *Diary*, 647). Are you praying for your priest prior to stepping into the confessional, or are you criticizing him and others, even gossiping as you are waiting in the confessional line? It might help to start praying for your confessor instead.

Once inside the confessional, people sometimes say something to this effect: "Father, I haven't been to Confession in 25 years, but I really don't have any sins." Here, the first sin to confess might be pride, because we are all sinners. Remember, Ven. Pope Pius XII said the greatest sin of the 20th century is the loss of the sense of sin. We seem to have lost humility. "I'm not a sinner. I'm fine. God would never, ever let me be lost." We can't be that presumptuous! Yes, God "desires all men to be saved and come to the knowledge of the truth" (1 Tim 2:4), but we also have the greatest gift of free will, so your choices can condemn you. That happens when we have blindness toward our own sins and rarely worry about their consequences. Perhaps this happens more frequently today because concern about sin has almost disappeared in our world. Watching TV or listening to the radio, it seems sin has lost all its seriousness. Politicians, actors, and professional athletes use the most vulgar language, words you would never imagine hearing just a few years ago. Since we have become desensitized, nobody seems to think there's anything wrong with it any more. We've become completely oblivious to the fact that sin exists and how serious it is. We need to wake up. Saint Faustina wrote, "I learned in the depths of my soul how horrible sin was, even the smallest sin, and how much it tormented the soul of Jesus. I would rather suffer a thousand hells than commit even the smallest venial sin" (*Diary*, 1016).

Is Your Confession Valid?

It is prudent to mention here that just because one goes to Confession, it doesn't mean they are automatically forgiven of their sins. That may sound counterintuitive, but your Confession may be invalid if it is missing any one of three necessary components. First, you must confess all grave sins you can remember. What about sins that you cannot remember? If you have honestly forgotten them, then yes, they are forgiven. However, don't play games and have "selective memory" because God knows if you honestly forgot or were rather just embarrassed to confess a certain sin. Please know that if you are aware of even one grave sin and you purposely don't confess it because you are embarrassed or feel you were justified in committing it, your current Confession is invalid and none of your sins are forgiven; moreover, if you continue to omit that sin in the confessional, then *all* subsequent Confessions are invalid as well!

One interesting fact is that Martin Luther, whom most people believe left the Church for its selling of indulgences (there's more to the story on that issue, too), actually left the Church because of his own fear. Yes, he would spend hours in the confessional, almost daily, and was so obsessed with trying to remember every transgression he committed that he believed that he would go to hell if he didn't confess every single sin, even venial ones.[46] However, this is not Catholic Church teaching. This dilemma pierced Luther's soul, and he could never come to terms with it. What a shame that he ended up leaving the Catholic Church and changing the world because he simply didn't understand Catholic teaching.

The second condition needed for a Confession to be valid is that you must have some form of contrition. If someone is forcing you to be in the confessional and you really don't have anything in your heart that says, "I'm sorry," then your Confession is not valid. You must have at least a bit of contrition in your heart, which is sorrow that you have offended the Almighty God, Creator and Sustainer of your life and the universe. We should reiterate here that even the most imperfect form of contrition —simply the fear of hell, for example — is far from ideal but still enough to fulfill the condition needed for a valid Confession. In addition, we need to have a firm purpose of amendment, which is honest intent not to repeat the sin(s).

The third condition we must fulfill for a valid Confession is that we must do penance (or some form of satisfaction), which is something the priest will tell you to do sometime before your next Confession. This could include something as simple as a heartfelt prayer, such as an Our Father or Hail Mary, or it could be longer prayers such as praying a Rosary or Chaplet of Divine Mercy for a particular intention. Penances could also include an act of kindness, especially for someone you have hurt, or a denial of yourself, such as fasting from something you enjoy. However, the penance must have a point of completion. A very good friend of mine was assigned a penance by a local priest to pray an Our Father *every day* for the rest of his life for a deceased family member he had trouble forgiving. Although my friend has continued to do this, and the intent of both the priest and penitent was admirable, this would *not* be a proper penance and the person has the right to ask for a different penance.

And if you forget your penance after you leave the confessional, which has happened to me more than once, during your next Confession you may ask the priest for an additional penance, or choose something yourself that you feel is appropriate for the sins you've committed. Now if you have embezzled hundreds of thousands of dollars from a charity, cheated on your taxes, and had an affair, one Hail Mary is probably not enough!

So, to summarize: What are the acts of the penitent needed for a valid Confession?

1. *Confession,* which consists in the telling of at least one's mortal sins to the priest, so this should have included an examination of conscience with the Ten Commandments or the Seven Deadly Sins;

2. *Contrition* (or repentance), which is perfect when it is motivated by love of God, and imperfect (but still valid) if it rests on other motives and that includes the determination not to sin again; and

3. *Satisfaction,* or the carrying out of certain acts of penance that the confessor imposes upon the penitent to repair the damage caused by sin.

Sin and Temporal Punishment

Once you have completed a valid Confession, you are now completely forgiven of the eternal punishment resulting from sin: hell. However, temporal punishment for your sins may remain on your soul. Yes, Jesus did everything for our redemption on the Cross, so that Heaven is now open to all who desire it, but not everyone is ready to go through the door to Heaven — hence, the fitting Catholic (and scriptural) doctrine of Purgatory. Purgatory is not for the forgiveness of grave sins (that is done in Confession) but rather it is a place to prepare to meet God — much like a bride prepares herself before the wedding (without seeing the groom) to finally see him, looking as beautiful as she can in pure white. Purgatory is a place of *purification* from past sins, *detachment* from things in our life (sinful and non-sinful) that we may not have done before we died, and *preparation* to meet God. But this "punishment" is only temporal, as every soul in Purgatory will eventually be in Heaven. Remember, Holy Souls (*holy* meaning they are on their way to Heaven) cannot pray for themselves, and only you and I can pray for them to relieve their temporal punishment.

One good visual explanation of temporal punishment is the hammer, nail, and wood example. You hammer the nail, which is like your sin, into a block of wood, which is like the world. Absolution in Confession removes the nail, the sin, but a hole remains in the wood (the world) that needs to be repaired. Jesus never promised to dismiss us from the consequences of our sins, so we need to make reparation to God's justice for the wrongs we have done. Remember, Christ dying on the Cross did not take away God's justice. It still remains. Think of it this way: A loving father reminds his son not to play baseball in the front yard of their home, in fear that a window will be broken. Disobeying this "commandment," the boy doesn't think anything will happen (as we often think regarding our sins) but in fact, this is dangerous. In this case, the ball sails through the window and shatters it. The father comes home and forgives his son and confirms his love for the boy, but informs him that he is grounded and will pay for it out of his allowance. In essence, he has been lovingly "punished" on a temporary basis. That is why I prefer the term "loving discipline," as it is God as a Father lovingly correcting us as His wayward children.

Thus, temporal punishment, the residual effect of your sin, may remain even after our sins are forgiven in Confession, meaning reparation must be offered for the damage we have done to the Body of Christ. One great way to do that is through plenary indulgences, which are actions we can do to seek remission of the temporal punishment for sins already confessed, as long as we meet the ordinary conditions (detachment from all sin, sacramental Confession, Holy Communion, and prayer for the intentions of the Holy Father). So seek opportunities for a plenary indulgence for yourself, or for the remaining temporal punishment a soul in Purgatory may have to endure, especially if you are part of the reason they are in Purgatory!

It's exciting to know, however, that there is another way to remit this temporal punishment that we are owed, a way even greater than a plenary indulgence. Yes, Jesus offers an incredible grace, an *Extraordinary Promise*, on Divine Mercy Sunday, which is the Sunday after Easter Sunday. On this day, Jesus offers every soul the opportunity for complete forgiveness of sins and all punishment, if we simply go to Confession and receive Holy Communion on that day. (Confession can be done sometime before, as long as you are in a state of grace when receiving Holy Communion on Divine Mercy Sunday.)[47] It is not some magic words or crazy promise; it is simply Christ's way to get us back to the Sacraments so that we can become spotless, without blemish. We can do that through the rays of Divine Mercy: the pale ray, which is the cleansing waters of Baptism and Confession, and the red ray, the life-giving Precious Blood of Holy Communion. This is fully explained in my book *Understanding Divine Mercy*, so please don't miss this grace!

We should all strive to receive the Eucharist without sin on our soul. But how? Aren't we all sinners? Yes, so how are we to "reconcile" this (pun intended)? We can be "spotless" by simply following the teaching of the Church. If we have grave sin on our soul, we are required to go to

Confession prior to receiving Holy Communion at Mass. But the Church does not teach that we have to confess all of our venial sins, which are still sins, so what about those? Yes, those are stains on our soul. Seem confusing? Not really. That's because venial sins are washed away in the Mass! Yes, if you have gone to Confession for grave sin, and you attend Mass from the start (especially the Penitential Rite, and blessing yourself with holy water), even your slightest sins are gone. Thus, you are spotless at the moment you receive Holy Communion without bringing condemnation upon yourself, as St. Paul warns us: "Whoever, therefore, eats the bread or drinks the cup of the Lord in an unworthy manner will be guilty of profaning the body and blood of the Lord. Let a man examine himself, and so eat of the bread and drink of the cup. For any one who eats and drinks without discerning the body eats and drinks judgment upon himself. That is why many of you are weak and ill, and some have died" (1 Cor 11:27-30).

Remember, all of this assumes that you have made a valid Confession, meaning you've confessed all the grave sins that you can remember; you've had some form of contrition and you're sorry, even if it isn't perfect; and you do some form of penance to atone for the damage your sins have caused the Body of Christ. We need Confession, and God tells how to receive forgiveness on His terms. Saint Paul says, "All of this is from God, who through Christ, reconciled us to himself and gave us the ministry of reconciliation" (2 Cor 5:18). Since this comes from God, we would expect the effects to be powerful — and they are. The effects of the Sacrament of Reconciliation (*Catechism*, 1496) are:

- Forgiveness of sins and therefore reconciliation with God.
- Reconciliation with the Church.
- Recovery, if it has been lost, of the state of grace.

- Remission of the eternal punishment merited by mortal sins (hell).
- Remission, at least in part, of the temporal punishment which is the consequence of sin.
- Peace, serenity of conscience, and spiritual consolation.
- An increase of spiritual strength for the struggle of Christian living (more grace).

Are All Sins Forgivable?

It is true that God's mercy is greater than any sin, but is every sin forgivable? There's only one sin that Jesus says is unforgivable: "Whoever blasphemes against the Holy Spirit can never have forgiveness, but is guilty of an eternal sin" (Mk 3:29). It's about rejecting God, not asking for His mercy, and having, Jesus says, "an unclean spirit," or the devil. "Oh my gosh, Father! How do I make sure that I am not guilty of *that* sin?" Not to worry: By the very fact that you are sorry for all your sins and are seeking His Mercy, you cannot be guilty of this sin. As long as you know God has the power to forgive your sins, and you don't consciously align with the evil one, you can't be guilty of this sin. As long as you don't despair and think your sins are greater than God's mercy, you can't be guilty of this sin. The very fact that you walk into the confessional with the intent to make a valid Confession, you are asking for God's mercy and cannot be guilty of this sin.

On the contrary, if we despair and think our sins are bigger than God's mercy, or we are presumptuous, thinking God is so merciful that He would never send us to hell (God doesn't send us to hell; we send ourselves by our choices), then we can put ourselves into a bind. But even then it is not too late to turn back to God's mercy in Confession!

Saint Faustina wrote that if you took all the sins ever committed in the history of the world and put them together, they would be just a drop compared to the ocean that is God's mercy (*Diary*, 835). And what about, "Father, I don't go to Confession because God will not listen to me. He hates me. You have no idea what I've done." If God truly hated you, He would not have created you and you would not be in existence today. I can prove that God loves you and wants to forgive you by the fact that you are reading this book right now.

Thus, the only unforgivable sin is putting yourself outside the mercy of God. Well, what about those who don't deserve God's mercy? Jesus said the *sinner* has a greater right to His mercy than even the *righteous* person. Wow — that is hard to comprehend in one sense, but on the other hand it shouldn't be. I come from a military family and my father was in Vietnam. On the battlefield, who do you think has a greater right to the medic: the man who pricked his finger on a shell casing and was slightly bleeding, or the guy who had his whole arm blown off by a mortar shell and was hemorrhaging to death? Of course, the one closer to death has the first right to the medic. When you're a sinner, you're closer to death; thus you have the greater right to God's mercy (see St. Faustina, *Diary*, 423).

Scripture confirms this. Saint Paul tells us our sinfulness cannot prevent us from receiving God's mercy. He knew this personally, as he wrote to Timothy, "Christ Jesus came into the world to save sinners — of whom I am the foremost. But for that very reason I received mercy, so that in me, as the foremost, Jesus Christ might display the utmost patience, making me an example to those who would come to believe in him for eternal life" (1 Tim 1:15-16). Only our fear and refusal to trust Him (the only unforgivable sin) prevents us from receiving Divine Mercy. Pope Francis said God never tires of forgiving; we just tire of asking for forgiveness. Remember, the only way your soul is going to be lost is by dying in an unrepentant state of mortal sin. Confession is so important because it prohibits that from happening.

Summary of Why We Need Confession

So why do we need Confession? Because it's either shame or salvation. Take your pick. Sorry to be graphic, but don't you feel much better after you vomit, after you get all that junk out? In the same way, you will feel much better when you get the junk of sin and vice out of your soul, and this is what Confession does. In Confession, you have a mini spiritual resurrection. Your soul was dead if you were in mortal sin because Christ cannot dwell in your soul, but in Confession, God comes back in and you have now been resurrected. Christ conquered death on the Cross, and now He gives you the chance to conquer the death of your soul in the Sacrament of Reconciliation. So go to Confession. As consecrated religious, our priests and brothers go every two weeks, no matter what the state of their soul is. Perhaps going at least once a month (like on First Saturdays) is a good habit for you to consider. Actually, it's one of the healthiest habits you can adopt.

A 2024 poll revealed that 42 percent of Catholics surveyed said they go to Confession once a year — compared to just 10 percent in a 2022 survey.[48] This is encouraging, but still not enough! Priests must remind the world that sin exists, not in a dreary and depressing manner, but with an attitude of joy and enthusiasm because forgiveness is only a confessional door away! This paves the way for any other sacramental encounters that increase the divine life within us. Once the roadblock of sin is removed, then the process of God transforming your life (divinization) can begin, and only then.[49] Remember, at our judgment, Satan can only accuse us of unconfessed sins, so take away all of his ammo!

Jesus heals the body in Anointing of the Sick (our next section), and He heals the soul in Confession. These are the Sacraments of Healing. Christ, the Physician of our body and soul, instituted these Sacraments because the new life that He gives us in the Sacraments like Baptism can be weakened and even lost because of sin. Christ willed His Church to continue His work of healing and salvation by means of Anointing and Confession. The new life of grace received in Baptism does not abolish the weakness of human nature, nor the inclination to sin (that is, *concupiscence*). So, we can return to the Sacrament of Reconciliation whenever needed — this is incredible! That is why repeat Confessions are okay. As one mystic said, "Saints are simply sinners who keep on trying." The angels didn't get this opportunity — they had one chance to choose God because they could see the full effects of their choice. We fully don't, but we should have the full desire to want to choose God, even if we have to try and try again. And if we are too sick to go to the Confessional, God accounts for that as well by giving us the Sacrament of Anointing of the Sick.

Anointing of the Sick

> By the sacred anointing of the sick and the prayer of the priests the whole Church commends those who are ill to the suffering and glorified Lord, that he may raise them up and save them. And indeed she exhorts them to contribute to the good of the People of God by freely uniting themselves to the Passion and death of Christ.
>
> — *Catechism of the Catholic Church*, 1499

People tend to panic when a priest is called to the hospital for an anointing. The patient thinks the priest is the angel of death, coming to give Last Rites. For loved ones, it means Grandma is surely going to die, and then poor Grandma has an anxiety attack. But the Sacrament of Anointing of the Sick (also called Sacrament of the Sick) is something everyone eventually will need. It is given to those near death, or facing the possibility of death, such as going under anesthesia before a serious operation. The Sacrament of Anointing is not just for bodily or physical healing, but emotional and spiritual healing as well. Anointing imparts gifts of strengthening in the Holy Spirit against anxiety, discouragement, and temptations, uniting the person's suffering to Christ's suffering on the Cross, and gives peace and fortitude (*Catechism*, 1520). This is powerful healing. So, the priest is coming to see Grandma because we're praying for her healing, not necessarily to send her away. God decides the time, so please try to put her at ease. The *Catechism* states clearly that this is "not a sacrament for those only who are at the point of death. Hence, as soon as anyone of the faithful begins to be in danger of death from sickness or old age, the fitting time for him to receive this sacrament has already arrived" (1514). This is telling us to consider the Sacrament even before death is imminent; thus, have no fear, this is not a surrender to death. Anointing is a hope that God may bring healing. Keep in mind, however, that every time God does allow suffering, He wants to bring a greater good out of it, so there is meaning to what many see as evil. Suffering, therefore, can be redemptive.

Form, Matter, Minister

The celebration of this Sacrament should, if possible, be preceded by Confession. That is why the Sacrament can only be administered by a priest or bishop, the *minister*, because the major effect is tied to the ministry of the priest, the forgiveness of sins. The *matter* of the Sacrament is the Oil of the Sick that has been blessed by a bishop using this prayer:

> Lord God, all comforting Father, you brought healing to the sick through your Son Jesus Christ. Hear us as we pray to you in faith, and send the Holy Spirit, the Comforter, from heaven upon this oil, which nature has provided to serve the needs of men. May your blessing come upon all who are anointed with this oil, that they may be freed from pain, illness, and disease, and made well again in body, mind, and soul. Father, may this oil which you have blessed for our use produce its healing effect, in the name of our Lord Jesus Christ.

The *form* of the anointing is the spoken words of the prayer of the priest: "Through this holy anointing, may the Lord, in His love and mercy, help you with the grace of the Holy Spirit. May the Lord free you from sin, save you, and raise you up." The anointing prepares the sick person for the ultimate journey to the Father's House, which may be close.

You can certainly see what Jesus was doing when He instituted the seven Sacraments that we read in the Bible — everything ties together through the amazing grace of God. Remember how I said Confirmation completes Baptism? Well, Anointing of the Sick completes Confession. As we discussed, when we go to Confession, our sins are forgiven, but temporal punishment may remain. Anointing, when part of the Apostolic Pardon (as we will discuss shortly), completes the Sacrament of Reconciliation because it removes that residual temporal punishment that may still be on the soul. In this case, it's like the grace of Divine Mercy Sunday, which is a great day because you don't have to be sick or under anesthesia to receive the grace![50] In a way, it "goes beyond" Confession. For instance, when the person receiving the anointing does not have a chance to make a sacramental Confession (for example, if they lapsed into unconsciousness), but the priest has good reason to believe that the person would have asked for that Sacrament if they had been able to do so, the anointing guarantees that the soul will be forgiven and not be eternally lost.

Anointing of the Sick in Scripture

Jesus instituted the Anointing of the Sick during His public ministry when He sent forth His apostles: "He called the twelve and began to send them out two by two, and gave them authority over the unclean spirits. ... So they went out and proclaimed that all should repent. They cast out many demons, and anointed with oil many who were sick and cured them" (Mk 6:7, 12-13). As we discussed in the section on Confession, St. James also states, "Is anyone among you sick? He should summon the presbyters of the church, and they should pray over him and anoint [him] with oil in the name of the Lord, and the prayer of faith will save the sick person, and the Lord will raise him up" (Jas 5:14).[51]

As the Catholic faith teaches, we want to always pray for healing so that we can praise God if it happens — but as we said we also want to praise God by accepting suffering if it is redemptive for a soul, because suffering isn't always evil when God brings a greater good from it. Sometimes God is using our suffering to help others. Remember what St. Paul told the Galatians: "You know that it was because of a physical infirmity that I first announced the gospel to you; though my condition put you to the test, you did not scorn or despise me, but welcomed me as an angel of God, as Christ Jesus" (Gal 4:13-14). Had St. Paul not become ill, he would have continued on his journey and never had the chance to preach to the Galatians. This is just one example of how God uses suffering to accomplish His will. Therefore, if we suffer, we should look upon it as an opportunity for good, such as by offering up our sufferings for our own sanctification and for that of our departed brothers and sisters in Purgatory.[52]

The early Church Fathers recognized the role of the Sacrament of Anointing in the life of the Church. Around A.D. 250, Origen wrote that the penitent Christian "does not shrink from declaring his sin to a priest of the Lord and from seeking medicine," citing St. James: "Let them impose hands upon him, anointing him with oil in the name of the Lord; and the prayer of faith will save the sick man, and if he be in sins, they shall be forgiven him."[53] I often think of one of my heroes, St. Maximilian Kolbe, who ministered to his fellow prisoners in the Nazi concentration camp in Auschwitz before his martyrdom. Although there is no evidence he had access to Oil of the Sick to anoint, he heard Confessions and often celebrated Mass using smuggled-in bread and wine, providing strength and peace to help others spiritually prepare for death. Father Kolbe was undoubtedly an instrument of God's healing presence amid the horrors of war. "A single act of love makes the soul return to life," he wrote.[54]

When to Receive This Sacrament

So, who can be anointed, when, and how often? This is hugely confusing to many. Any member of the faithful can receive this Sacrament as soon as he or she begins to be in danger of death because of sickness or old age. It can also be given to someone going under anesthesia, as there is always the danger of not waking up. And a person can be anointed again if the illness worsens or another serious sickness afflicts them. The *Catechism* states:

> If a sick person who received this anointing recovers his health, he can in the case of another grave illness receive this sacrament again. If during the same illness the person's condition becomes more serious, the sacrament may be repeated. It is fitting to receive the Anointing of the Sick just prior to a serious operation. The same holds for the elderly whose frailty becomes more pronounced (1515).

Perhaps you are diagnosed with cancer and are anointed, but then the cancer goes to a new stage. In this case, you may be anointed again. The lingering effects of Lyme disease or long COVID are two other good examples that allow for anointing. You do not have to be dying, but your condition should be serious. And even if someone is unconscious, a priest can anoint conditionally, believing that they would accept this grace if they were awake and alert. So, please don't forget to call the priest for your loved one!

And please be careful not to overuse this Sacrament. It should not be given out like party favors. For example, some people go to Healing Masses on a regular basis, believing they are getting the Sacrament of Anointing every week. First of all, to receive an anointing that often would almost never be proper. That is why Healing Masses offer *blessings* rather than the Sacrament of Anointing (the word *anointing* means "blessing"). At a Healing Mass, like the ones we celebrate often at the National Shrine of The Divine Mercy in Stockbridge, Massachusetts, the priest makes the Sign of the Cross on foreheads with oil. This is a blessing, not a Sacrament, because the words in the rite of the Sacrament are not pronounced and the Oil of the Sick blessed by the bishop at the Chrism Mass is not used. Moreover, this Sacrament cannot be abused or the grace is ineffective. For example, Canon law states that the Anointing of the Sick "is not to be conferred upon those who persevere obstinately in manifest grave sin," unless they show repentance (1007). This is something we should keep in mind when requesting the Sacrament for our loved ones.

Can non-Catholics receive the Anointing of the Sick? That depends. Baptism is the gateway to all Sacraments, so we can't anoint someone who hasn't been baptized. The person must also be open to confessing the faith and have a desire matching Catholic belief.[55]

Last Rites?

Anointing of the Sick is one of the three Sacraments, along with Reconciliation and Holy Eucharist, that make up what we call Extreme Unction, or more commonly *Last Rites*. These are the Sacraments given to people on their deathbed to prepare them to meet God at the gates of Heaven. The most important part of Last Rites is the reception of the Lord in Holy Communion. This is called *Viaticum*, which in Latin means "take on the road," like "food for the journey." The *Catechism* emphasizes the importance of Last Rites:

> The Christian who unites his own death to that of Jesus views it as a step towards him and an entrance into everlasting life. When the Church for the last time speaks Christ's words of pardon and absolution over the dying Christian, seals him for the last time with a strengthening anointing,

and gives him Christ in viaticum as nourishment for the journey, she speaks with gentle assurance: "Go forth, Christian soul, from this world. ... May you see your Redeemer face to face" (1020).

How beautiful. Now, if someone has already died, the administration of Last Rites is not possible. But what about Anointing of the Sick? The Church teaches that the moment of death is when the soul leaves the body, but the problem is we don't always know exactly when that occurs. So, if the body is still warm and there's no evidence of stiffening like *rigor mortis*, if the priest has reasonable doubt that the person is still partly alive, he can administer a conditional anointing. If in fact the person is dead, and *rigor mortis* has set in, the priest then prays for the deceased, asking God to forgive that person's sins and receive that person into His kingdom. In this case, he should *not* do an anointing.

I cannot emphasize enough the importance of calling for a priest when your loved one is near death, in the hospital, or at home in hospice care. So many times the priest is called after the loved one has died, and there's not much he can do beyond prayers of comfort. So be prepared, because the Last Rites are vital! Alert your parish of your loved one's grave condition, and find out how to contact your parish priest in an emergency. If the hospital has a Catholic chaplain on call, find out how he can be reached at a moment's notice.

And when the priest does come, don't forget to ask for a very important grace given through the authority of the Church: *The Apostolic Pardon*. This brings total forgiveness of punishment before death because it is a blessing and indulgence given to a dying Catholic in the state of grace. It is part of the Last Rites and is intended to prepare the person for death. Here I refer to the explanation given by our friends at Catholic Answers, which is always a great go-to source for accurate information on the faith:

The Apostolic Pardon is blessing with an indulgence that happens at the conclusion of the Anointing of the Sick if the recipient is in danger of death. The usual process is Confession, then Anointing of the Sick, and it is concluded with the Apostolic Pardon. While Confession forgives the eternal punishment for sin, the indulgence attached to the Apostolic Pardon forgives temporal punishment due to sin. The words of the blessing said by the priest for the Apostolic Pardon are: "Through the holy mysteries of our redemption, may almighty God release you from all punishments in this life and in the life to come. May He open to you the gates of paradise and welcome you to everlasting joy" or "By the authority which the Apostolic See has given me, I grant you a full pardon and the remission of all your sins in the name of the Father, and of the Son, and of the Holy Spirit."[56]

May you and your loved ones find added peace in this great gift to souls who are on their deathbed. With the Apostolic Pardon, you can have confidence that you have done all you could do to bring the soul of a loved one closer to the gates of Heaven.

Lastly, in addition to conferring the Sacrament, one of the best means of assisting a dying person is the one that Jesus revealed to St. Faustina and insisted that she use often, even continuously: the Chaplet of the Divine Mercy. Jesus said, **"My daughter, encourage souls to say the chaplet which I have given to you. It pleases Me to grant everything they ask of Me by saying the chaplet. ... Write that when they say this chaplet in the presence of the dying, I will stand between My Father and the dying person, not as the just Judge but as the merciful Savior"** (*Diary*, 1541). Earlier, our Lord said to her, **"At the hour of their** death, I defend as My own glory every soul that will say this chaplet; or when others say it for a dying person, the indulgence is the same" (*Diary*, 811).

Saint Faustina was often given the grace to know when a certain dying person desired or needed prayer; she would be alerted to the moment by her Guardian Angel or by our Lord Himself. At those times she would pray until she no longer felt the need to pray, or a sense of peace came upon her, or she learned that the person had died, or heard the soul say, "Thank you!" She wrote, "Oh, dying souls are in such great need of prayer! O Jesus, inspire souls to pray often for the dying" (*Diary*, 1015).[57]

So, whenever you hear about someone who is sick and in danger of dying, pray the Chaplet of Divine Mercy for them. Even if the dying person lives far away, your prayers still count (see *Diary*, 835). Moreover, don't think you could ever miss your chance to pray for someone who has already died, as it's never too late to pray the Chaplet for them. God is outside of time, and He will hear your prayers no matter when they are offered for someone.

Though this fallen world is filled with sadness and death, goodness really does have the final say. We just need to do our part and pray for others — especially for those who are dying.

THE SACRAMENTS OF SERVICE

Holy Orders

> Holy Orders is the sacrament through which the mission entrusted by Christ to his apostles continues to be exercised in the Church until the end of time; thus it is the sacrament of apostolic ministry. It includes three degrees: episcopate, presbyterate [priest], and diaconate.
>
> — *Catechism of the Catholic Church*, 1536

There are priests in most religions, including Judaism, where priests were seen as mediators between God and men. They instructed people, sanctified them, and offered sacrifices on their behalf. Then Jesus came along and changed everything. In Christianity there is only one priest: Jesus Christ. Just like other priests, Christ instructed the people, sanctified them, and offered sacrifice. But He did all of this in such a perfect way that nothing can actually be added to it. Jesus is the perfect mediator, and no wonder, being True God and True Man. Since He rose from the dead, He dies no more. So, if there's only one single High Priest in the New Covenant, Jesus Christ, who are all these men in black shirts, suits, and robes? Who are Catholic priests, and are they really needed?

Well, it's like this. Jesus offered the perfect sacrifice on the Cross at Calvary. He gave up His life out of love for mankind in order that the sacrifice of the Cross may remain always present and continue to sanctify mankind. Jesus instituted the Sacrament of the Eucharist at the Last Supper, which we call the Sacrifice of the Mass. What Catholics do at Holy Mass is not a new sacrifice, but rather the making present of the one Sacrifice on the Cross. The priest offering the Sacrifice of the Mass is indeed Christ Himself, *in persona Christi* (in the person of Christ), when he is at the altar. Christ is the One being sacrificed and the One who offers the sacrifice. Everything that happens at Mass isn't just something purely spiritual, but a Sacrament that is a visible sign instituted by Christ. And if in the Holy Eucharist the sacrifice is represented through the species of bread and wine, then the one who performs the consecration should also be represented in some physical way. This is precisely what the sacramental priesthood does.

Surprisingly, the priest's first function as a shepherd of souls is not to bring the people, his "sheep," to eternal existence through teaching, admonition through sermons, or even prayer. The priest's first function is the Sacraments! God the Father gives all power to the Son, who then gives it to the priests to act in His name. Now the priest as Christ's representative on earth has the same power on earth as Christ did (the priest is *not* His replacement — there is a big difference). Christ had to ascend to the Father, so how is He made present today? By the priest. All other priests in history, including in the Old Testament and even medicine men, offered a sacrifice apart from themselves.

For instance, the Jews believed sin was so ingrained in the human condition it was even in the blood; so, the shedding of blood represented the emptying of sin. The priest and victim (an animal, like a goat) were very distinct and separate, but not now with Jesus (and now with the priest). Everything has changed. The essence of the Old Covenant was that the priest offered a sacrifice of blood in expiation for sin, which is why we have the term "scapegoat," as an innocent being had to be killed, and blood shed, for the sins of the people. This is because the penalty for sin is death; but the High Priest, Jesus, not the goat, now pays that debt and the priest stands in His stead.

The ordained priest is there in order to represent Christ, to make Christ present and visible to the people. The ordained priest doesn't act in his own name, but acts as Christ through his ordination. He participates in the one priesthood of Christ, as he is consecrated into the one priesthood of Christ. This makes the priest in the Catholic understanding completely different from the "priest" in any other religion. As Jesus told St. Faustina, **"When you approach the confessional, know this, that I Myself am waiting there for you. I am only hidden by the priest, but I Myself act in your soul"** (*Diary*, 1602).

Form, Matter, Minister

The Sacrament of Holy Orders, along with the Sacrament of Matrimony, are Sacraments of Service, as they are "directed toward the salvation of others" and "confer a particular mission in the Church and serve to build up the People of God" (*Catechism*, 1534). Through the Sacrament of Holy Orders, men become deacons, priests, and bishops, in that order. The hierarchy of the Sacrament dictates that, in order to be ordained a priest, one must first be ordained a deacon, and in order to become a bishop, one must have already been ordained a priest. Laymen can be admitted to the first degree, the permanent diaconate. Men who are pursuing a vocation to the priesthood are ordained as "transitional" deacons.

There are two paths to priesthood, each with different types of formation and training. A man can apply to the bishop of a diocese to enter a diocesan vocation program. Diocesan priests make promises (not vows) of poverty, chastity, and obedience. They serve in parishes and in diocesan institutions such as Catholic schools and Catholic charities. They do not usually live in community, but rather in individual parishes, so this is the type of priest most commonly known to the laity.

A man can also choose the religious life and apply to a congregation or order such as the Marian Fathers of the Immaculate Conception. The formation program is longer (averaging 6-10 years) and more regimented, with a candidate passing through different levels, first as a postulant, then a novice, then temporary vows, before making perpetual or "final" vows of poverty, chastity, and obedience. Depending on the "rule" of the religious order, priests may minister in the world (often within dioceses) and live in community, or live a cloistered life of prayer. The former is referred to as an apostolic community, while the latter is referred to as a cloistered community. However, the Sacrament of Holy Orders is the same for every new priest, whether being ordained for a diocese or for a religious order.

The *Catechism* states that ordination "confers a gift of the Holy Spirit that permits the exercise of a 'sacred power' (*sacra potestas*) which can come only from Christ himself through his Church. Ordination is also called *consecratio*, for it is a setting apart and an investiture by Christ himself for his Church" (1538). Ordinations take place during a Mass, preferably at a cathedral, and the *minister* is the ordaining bishop, archbishop, cardinal, or pope. The *matter* of Holy Orders consists of the laying on of hands by this minister on the head of the candidate, and the *form* is the prayer he recites, the solemn prayer of consecration. With this prayer he asks God on behalf of the candidate for the special outpouring of the Holy Spirit and for the gifts of the Spirit proper to the ministry (deacon, priest, bishop) to which he is being ordained. The anointing of the new priest's hands with sacred chrism seals the priest with an indelible, spiritual character that configures him to Christ the High Priest and enables him to act in His Name. Ordination is permanent and cannot be repeated or conferred for a limited time. "You are a priest forever according to the order of Melchizedek" (Ps 110:4; Heb 7:17).

The Priesthood in Scripture

Who was Melchizedek mentioned in the Bible, and what is his significance? Melchizedek was a priest during the Age of Patriarchs. He blessed Abraham and received a tithe from him, which means that he was greater than Abraham, our father in faith, and Abraham's descendants, Levi and David:

> And Melchizedek king of Salem brought out bread and wine; he was priest of God Most High. And he blessed him and said, "Blessed be Abram by God Most High, maker of heaven and earth; and blessed be God Most High, who has delivered your enemies into your hand!" And Abram gave him one-tenth of everything (Gen 14:18-20).

Melchizedek, king of Salem (*Salem* means "peace," and *Jerusalem* means "city of peace"), was appointed a priest directly by God, as was Jesus. So, the original form of the priesthood was of the order of Melchizedek. Saint Paul describes Jesus as "a priest forever according to the order of Melchizedek" (Heb 6:20). The *Catechism* confirms this important connection:

> Everything that the priesthood of the Old Covenant prefigured finds its fulfillment in Christ Jesus, the "one mediator between God and men." The Christian tradition considers Melchizedek, "priest of God Most High," as a prefiguration of the priesthood of Christ, the unique "high priest after the order of Melchizedek"; "holy, blameless, unstained," "by a single offering he has perfected for all time those who are sanctified," that is, by the unique sacrifice of the cross (1544).

So, Christ predates all those Old Testament priests and kings because He comes from a special order that precedes those kings and priests. The Jews all believed that the messiah would be a king, not a priest; therefore, the Book of Hebrews is important because it is the only place where Jesus is called a priest, not just a king. Melchizedek is important because he was the king of Salem as we mentioned, but he was also the first to be given the title *kohen* (priest) in the Old Testament ("priest of God Most High"). Melchizedek also offers bread and wine (see Gen 14:18), prefiguring the offering of bread and wine as part of the priesthood of Christ in His Church.

Psalm 110 says Melchizedek is representative of the priestly line through which a king of David's line would come. It shows there will be a change in the Levitical priesthood of Aaron to the Melchizedekian priesthood of Christ, going from the sacrifice with the blood of animals to the sacrifice with the Blood of Christ. The law of Moses said only the male descendants of Aaron could be commissioned priests, but Melchizedek was appointed priest directly by God (the Aaronic priesthood is by descent and blood — it was automatic). Christ also was chosen directly by God. In Hebrews, Jesus is a priest in the order of Melchizedek because, like Melchizedek, He was not a descendant of Aaron, and thus would not qualify for the established Jewish priesthood. Rather, Jesus has a right to a priesthood predating the Jewish Aaronic priesthood — He was the Messiah and Son of God. Genesis implies that the order of Melchizedek is the patriarchal order of priesthood that functioned for many centuries before the ordination of Aaron. It is the original form of the priesthood! In fact, it is said to be "eternal." Since his genealogy is unknown, Melchizedek is a figure or "type" of Christ, who is eternal.

Note that priestly authority at that time was rooted in the family's authority structure; the father did the worship. Then the first-born son took over these ministerial duties. That is why it makes sense, as Dr. Scott Hahn believes, that Melchizedek may be Shem, the first-born son of Noah.[58] He was 465 years old at the time Abram (later named Abraham) was 75, so their lives did overlap, with the genealogy in Genesis showing Shem living past Abraham. Shem was given the priesthood (Hebrew, *kehuna*) by receipt of his father Noah's blessing. This form of priesthood is based on the natural order of the family in an earthly sense, and Christ now being the High Priest models the heavenly sense, where Jesus is the Father's first-born Son.

The confusion over Melchizedek being both king and priest is solved by knowing that Shem was also a progenitor of the Davidic monarchy. Shem was both priest and king. But what about Jesus? When Jesus first came, all knew Him as a prophet (a prophet is a teacher), then as a king (He entered Jerusalem triumphantly), then finally as a priest (the Last Supper). These are the three offices of Christ: Jesus is priest, prophet, and king. For most of the Old Testament, priests and kings came from different lines of families. Aaron and his descendants, who were the priests, came from the tribe of Levi. David and his descendants (including Christ) from the tribe of Judah were the kings (Messiah prophecy). But in the "order of Melchizedek," the first-born wears both of these crowns. Wow!

Moreover, the ministry of Melchizedek in Salem foreshadows the ministry of Christ in the heavenly Jerusalem. Bread and wine are the sacrifice, just like in the heavenly sanctuary where Jesus offers His Father His Body and Blood (see Hebrews 7, 9). The priesthood of Melchizedek is more effective because it required a single sacrifice, unlike the Levites who made endless sacrifices. So why is all this important? Because in Genesis, Melchizedek offers a sacrifice of bread and wine, like the Catholic priest does at every Mass. Bread and wine are the very elements offered in thanksgiving by Melchizedek the priest.

What about priestly ordination in Scripture? Turn to Acts of the Apostles and the story of Matthias (see Acts 1:12-26). Jesus didn't pick him to replace Judas — the other apostles did. They exercised the authority Christ gave them, and every time they ordained someone, they laid hands on him. So, Jesus laid hands on the apostles who then, in turn, laid hands on Matthias and other men, who, in turn, laid hands on other men — all the way down to every living priest today. As mentioned earlier, this is called *Apostolic Succession*. When I was ordained a priest in 2014, Bishop Martin Holley laid his hands on me, so I can be traced physically back, by laying on of hands, from Bishop Holley all the way to Jesus Christ Himself. That's mind-boggling! So, the apostles have successors today in Catholic priests and bishops, just as the apostles themselves were the successors of Jesus.

But how do we know that this priesthood was handed down from the Last Supper as Catholics claim? Among other reasons (beyond the scope of this book), we know that the apostles were ordained priests because Jesus washed their feet (Jn 13:14-15). This was done at the priestly ordinations of Aaron and his sons (see Ex 40:30-32). Christ ordained and then delegated the power to the apostles to be priests in His image.

Regarding the priest's confecting of the Eucharist, those words are also found in the Bible. This was so foundational to the founding of Christianity, that all Christians believed in the Real Presence for more than 1,500 years until the Reformation. Christ could not have used clearer, more explicit words than, "This is My Body." He did not say, "This is a *sign* of My Body," or "This *represents* My Body." Christ gave His priests the power to change bread and wine into His Body and Blood. He made the apostles priests by saying, "Do this in remembrance of Me." The *Catechism* states, "The command of Jesus to repeat his actions does not only ask us to remember Jesus and what He did. It is directed at the liturgical celebration, by the Apostles and their successors" (1341). The word "remembrance" (*anamnesis*), as Christ uses it, does not mean "to remember the past." Our "remembrance" of Christ's Passion, death, and Resurrection is used just as the Jewish people use it when celebrating the

Passover; it is *not* simply remembering and celebrating an event of the past, but actually entails making the event real and present now so that we can enter into and share in the Paschal Mystery of our salvation. At every Mass, you *are* in the Upper Room!

Call No Man "Father"?

Jesus said to the disciples and the crowd, "And call no one your father on earth, for you have one Father — the one in heaven" (Mt 23:9). So why are priests called "father"? Doesn't this contradict what Jesus commanded? I get this question all the time. It's related to the charge put forth often by Protestants who say there is no more priesthood because Jesus is the only High Priest. While it's true that Jesus is the one High Priest, the Bible tells us that from Jesus comes other priests: ministerial priests like me, and the *common* (or *royal*) priesthood, like you. In the words of St. Peter, "you are a chosen race, a royal priesthood, a holy nation, God's own people, in order that you may proclaim the mighty acts of him who called you out of darkness into his marvelous light" (1 Pet 2:9).

Jesus didn't mean to never say the word "father" or not to refer to someone as your earthly father. My goodness, what about the Fourth Commandment: Honor your father and your mother (Dt 5:16)? In the parable of the rich man and Lazarus, the former cried out, "*Father* Abraham, have mercy on me" (Lk 16:24). Stephen called religious leaders "fathers" (see Acts 7:2), as did Paul in Acts 22:1. Later, St. Paul told the Corinthians he was their spiritual *father*:

> I am not writing this to make you ashamed, but to admonish you as my beloved children. For though you might have ten thousand guardians in Christ, you do not have many fathers. Indeed, in Christ Jesus I became your father through the gospel. (1 Cor 4:14-15).

Based on these passages and the Ten Commandments, Jesus clearly did not mean to call *no one* "father" in an earthly sense. Jesus meant that there is only one creator, or one true Father, one "Abba" in Heaven in a supernatural sense. Jesus meant we are no longer under the covenant of the patriarchs (Abraham, Isaac, Jacob). We are now under the covenant of the one and only "Abba, the Father," but that doesn't mean we don't have earthly or spiritual fathers to lead us to Christ, who takes us to the one true Father, Abba.

A priest, like a father in the natural realm, gives life-giving seed. The difference is that his seed comes from the altar in the form of the Eucharist, and is received by the Church (*Mother* Church, the feminine) to bring about life. So, in that sense, a priest is a spiritual father to his congregation, and this is why we call priests "father." Through the administration of the Sacraments, priests impart grace in a supernatural way. A priest doesn't have to marry a woman to be a father, because his "bride" is the Church.

What About Married Priests or Women Priests?

This leads to the other big questions: *Why can't Catholic priests marry?* and *Why can't women be Catholic priests?* One of the things I struggled with when I thought about becoming a priest was the rule that I would not be able to marry. In fact, I delayed my vocation for many years in the hope that the Church would change her rule on married priests, which she can (unlike women's ordination) because this is just Church discipline, not dogma. My thought was that as soon as I get ordained, the Church will allow married men to be ordained; then it would be too late for me. (Remember, ordained men can *never* marry, so there is a difference.)

I was engaged to be married to a beautiful girl in North Carolina, and I thought it would have been great to have a family with her *and* be a priest. But now I see the wisdom in the Church's practice of having clergy live a celibate life. The campaign by some to end clerical celibacy is not fully informed. There is no way I could do what I do and be married, since it would always be unfair to both, with my wife and family only "getting me" 50 percent of the time, and the Church only "getting me" 50 percent of the time. A priest cannot have a "divided heart"; he cannot do everything and have two wives, so to speak. As priests, our "wife" is the Church.

Right now, my ministry normally lasts from 6 a.m. until midnight, seven days a week. In addition to my usual priestly duties — celebrating Mass, hearing Confessions, making sick calls, and so on — there are my administrative duties as provincial superior, such as intensive paperwork; but I also travel to speak at conferences and missions, and write talks for my Saturday *Explaining the Faith* series and our weekly EWTN program, *Living Divine Mercy*, and more. Praise God that I love this ministry or I would never be able to give the time and effort needed to persevere in this apostolic work. And please don't believe the common myth that if priests were allowed to marry, it would end the sex abuse problem. The true statistics paint a different picture: Most pedophiles are married men.[59]

What about the second question: *Why can't women be ordained to the priesthood?* First, Jesus came to earth as a man, and we can't change that. We had no determination in the fact that God chose to be incarnate as a man, so it's not sexist or anti-women. Please understand that the Church is not chauvinistic in not allowing women priests. Pope St. John Paul II stated clearly, "I declare that the Church has no authority whatsoever to confer priestly ordination on women and that this judgment is to be definitively held by all the Church's faithful."[60] If any woman could have been a priest, it would have been Jesus' own Mother, Mary — yet she was not a priest. The Church is just saying that there are rules given directly by God, and not even the Church can change them.

It's about the priest being *in persona Christi*, in the person of Christ, and Christ was a man. And that's who the priest is in all the sacramental acts of the Church. It is not the Church holding women down, because in this same Church, a cloistered nun is a higher vocational calling than a diocesan priest (although not higher in grace in the sense that only a priest can perform the Sacraments) because Jesus said Mary chose the better *contemplative* way over the busy, *apostolic* way of her sister Martha. "Martha, Martha, you are anxious and worried about many things," Jesus said. "There is need of only one thing. Mary has chosen the better part, which will not be taken away from her" (Lk 10:41-42). A cloistered nun has a way of life in imitation of the Blessed Virgin Mary, and thereby gives great glory to God in her vocation. This elevates the role of women in the Church, so the Church is not misogynistic or chauvinistic. To the Church, and to God, men and women are equal, but different.

Let's return to our brief statement earlier about the priest being called "father" because he produces life-giving seed from the altar in the form of the Eucharist. This also sheds light on the issue of women priests. As in the order of nature, the seed always comes from the male, is received by the female, then nurtured inside her, enabling her to give birth to new life. It is the same in the Mass. The priest gives that seed, in the form of the Eucharist, and it is received by the feminine, Holy Mother Church. This is why the Church has been referred to as *feminine* since its very inception 2,000 years ago.

As "Mother" Church (made of individual members), she receives that seed of the Eucharist from the priest at the altar and that seed is then nurtured in the person, who then goes out to give "birth" to new life: a new life in Christ. This mystical symbolism doesn't work if the person at the altar is a woman — a woman doesn't produce the seed, a man does. A woman receives the seed. Although our society wants to teach the contrary, this process is based on the order of nature, the difference between man and woman (although both are equal in dignity). So, the congregation (the feminine) is to live out that new life in Christ, but it takes a priest (the masculine, the *father*) to provide that living seed to generate that new life in Christ.

Surprisingly, It is Great Joy!

As should be clear by now, the life of a Catholic priest is a life of great joy. It's giving life and it is living out that life in the love of Jesus. The most awesome thing about the Catholic priesthood is that we make Christ present to the world. Many people talk about the things that a man must deny himself in order to be a priest, but there are many things that also attract one to the priesthood. The priesthood is a unique mission for which we need soldiers, real men — priests who can stand up and fight not just the evil one but secular society and the lies being taught to our Catholic faithful. The very future of the Church is at stake, making the priest an integral part of the parish and of society. Consider the wisdom of St. John Vianney:

> After God, the priest is everything. Leave a parish twenty years without priests; they will worship beasts. If the missionary Father and I were to go away, you would say, "What can we do in this church? There is no Mass; Our Lord is no longer there: we may as well pray at home." When people wish to destroy religion, they begin by attacking the priest, because where there is no longer any priest there is no sacrifice, and where there is no longer any sacrifice there is no religion.[61]

Parents, please encourage your young sons to be altar servers. Let them observe at close range the Eucharistic miracle performed by the priest, *in persona Christi*, at every Mass. And when the time comes to talk about your son's future and his vocational path, include the priesthood! We all know well about the vocational crisis and lack of priests in modern times, but this tide may be turning. A new generation of men now entering the priesthood is returning to the sense of the sacred in the Liturgy, in their pastoral duties, and in their teaching.

Father Donald Calloway, MIC, vocation director of the Marian Fathers, says he is seeing a boom in vocations (at least to our congregation and other good religious orders and dioceses with good bishops). He believes it is directly related to our order being faithful to the Truth and to Church teachings. We Marian priests are faithful to the Magisterium and to the office of the papacy. So, it is imperative that this trend of good new men entering the priesthood continue, because there is much damage to repair, such as that from the sex abuse scandal. Many people have abandoned their faith and now condemn the whole Church because of it. Justifiably, they ask, "How can a priest of God do such things?"

The Scandal

The priesthood is received from God; it is not chosen. I did not call myself; if I did, I would not have the grace to persevere in this vocation. So how, then, can abusive priests be men of God? Those involved in the scandal were actually called to be priests, but they rejected the grace, just like Judas did. People forget that Judas was called to the priesthood, but look what happened to him and so many other priests over time. There is *no* excuse for abusive priests, and abuse can never be hidden — everyone agrees that such priests need to be removed, and it is scandalous that some never were. It breaks Jesus' heart when those He calls, His priests, turn from His love. But because they did, the scandal actually needed to happen. You can either clean up your own house or someone else will. Like a cut, the wound has to be exposed to the air to be healed and purified.

As a result, many innocent priests are also suffering the effects of these sins. Remember, sin not only affects the person who commits it — it affects the entire Body of Christ. Now all priests (good and bad) and victims are going through the cross caused by the sin of this scandal. It is like Christ going through His Cross because of our sins. We are going through our cross because of their sins. Jesus told St. Faustina that the Bride must resemble her betrothed (*Diary*, 268). We, the Church, are the Bride (Jesus is the Groom); we are now in the Crucifixion phase of the scandal, and it hurts. Like Christ, we cannot expect to have Resurrection Sunday without going through the pains of Good Friday. Since the death of the last apostle, we are in the end times (although we do not know how long that will be).

So please also remember to pray for our new young men coming to the Marian Fathers to serve God, because it's not easy being a priest today, especially in light of the clergy abuse scandal. The world hates the priesthood more than ever because of what it represents: Jesus, the High Priest. Today there is a common disdain for the priesthood (many believe it's about money, molesters, and hypocrites) that Jesus warned about at the Last Supper, saying the world hated both He and the Father first, so the world will hate priests, too. We often see this hatred even more magnified when the priest acts in an unholy way.

Yes, some of this anger is understandable. Our Lord had justified anger at the moneychangers in the Temple, and this situation with abuse is much more serious. Thus, we should have justified anger at those priests who have abused children. There is no excuse. Until we have every single priest in this world living his vows faithfully and not abusing a single child, we will never stop being vigilant. We will always be transparent and cooperate with the authorities. If you are a victim of priest abuse, there are no words I can say to completely rectify the situation. All I can do, on behalf of the Church, is apologize and promise that, as provincial superior of a major religious order, along with all Church leadership, we are doing our best to address any issues that may put a child (or vulnerable adult) at risk.

As painful as all of this is for the laity, there is also pain for some priests who have been falsely accused, even imprisoned, yet who have been later found to be innocent. Unfortunately, there has been hurt on both sides, with real victims, but also falsely accused priests. While many cases of heinous crimes are real, some innocent priests have been charged with crimes they did not commit. I know two of them personally. So, we have to be careful about condemning the priesthood as a whole, as that brings sin upon ourselves. In fact, only 1 percent of Catholic priests have abused minors, a number that is still too high and completely unacceptable, but in the general population, the number of child abusers is 4 percent.[62] Studies have shown that about 90 percent of child sexual abuse is perpetrated by someone known and trusted by the child or the child's family members, and 85 percent of cases go unreported.[63] So statistically, a Catholic Church, believe it or not, is one of the safest places for your children. But of course, there should be no cases of any abuse! We only give those statistics to show that this is not just a Catholic priest problem, but a broken humanity problem.

History has always included a few bad priests, some even found in the Bible. Adam had a priestly role in the Garden, to tend and keep it as the Old Testament priests in Jerusalem were to tend and keep the Temple, but he failed in his responsibilities. Aaron, the first High Priest of the Israelites, led the people in idol worship of the golden bull. Jesus called Simon Peter "Satan." Judas Iscariot betrayed Jesus. The apostles all abandoned Jesus in Gethsemane. The Jewish priests at the time of Jesus didn't recognize Him and led the people in calling for His crucifixion. Simon Peter denied Jesus three times. Thomas didn't believe in the Resurrection. Only one of the apostles, St. John, stayed and didn't abandon Jesus at the Cross.

Throughout the history of the Church, we've had criminals in the priesthood mixed in with the great saints. One of the great reformers, St. Peter Damian (c. 1007-1072), wrote *The Book of Gomorrah* in response to sexual sins and crimes among the clergy of his day and the urgent need for reform. He appealed to Pope Leo IX, saying, "A certain most abominable and exceedingly disgraceful vice has grown in our region, and unless it is quickly met with the hand of strict chastisement, it is certain that the sword of divine fury is looming to attack, to the destruction of many."[64]

Jesus told us that there would be sheep and goats, good and bad, in the Church until the end of the world (see Mt 25:31-46), so priests being included should come as no surprise. Therefore, "No effort must be spared to create a culture able to prevent such situations from happening, but also to prevent the possibility of their being covered up and perpetuated," Pope Francis has said. "The pain of the victims and their families is also our pain, and so it is urgent that we once more reaffirm our commitment to ensure the protection of minors and of vulnerable adults."[65] Amen to that.

Again, if you have been a victim of clergy abuse, you are in my prayers. I offer Masses for victims of the Church because abuse is terrifying and unacceptable. And so, my heart goes out to you. I am in pain with you, especially if you or your children have been abused. God bless you.

Pray for Priests

Yes, priests are broken along with the rest of humanity, so they need your prayers. And those guilty priests involved in the scandal need your prayers in many ways as much as the victims do, because their souls are in most danger. We don't often think of praying for them, but we really need to because they are in most need of God's mercy after what they have done.

And please pray for the innocent priests as well, since they are shouldering the burden left behind in the wake of the scandal. After all, we are human, so we make mistakes, too. But we need these priests to persevere. Scripture tells us, "I will strike the shepherd, and the sheep will be scattered" (Mk 14:27). This is what's happening now. The evil one is pursuing priests, obviously more than ever, and more than anyone else. This is why priests need your help and your prayers. The snares and the traps that the evil one sets, he sets for all of us, but especially for the souls of priests.

Just before I was ordained, I went to an elderly Dominican priest for Confession. I told him I was going to be ordained the next day and he said, "Are you ready for this?"

Naively, I replied, "I think so."

He said, "Just remember, tomorrow night at this time, your Wanted poster will be in the post office of hell."

I recall saying, "Gee, thanks, Father!" but I realized he was right. After some reflection, something occurred to me: How valuable our souls must be, and how fierce the fight must be for your soul, if the evil one never stops pursuing it and the King of the Universe died for it.

One important question to ask is, *How can the laity help the Church have holy priests?* Of course, we must pray and fast for our priests, but also acknowledge their authority as fathers of our parish families and of our spiritual associations. On Father's Day, consider giving your priest a card — it helps more than you can imagine. Remember your parish priest at Christmas and Easter as well. And if they are like me, they love leftovers! Celebrate their birthday as a parish family or celebrate their ordination anniversary. And always pray for good, holy vocations. The renewal of the priesthood is taking place through Divine Mercy and Our Lady, the two spiritual gifts for our times. It is also Divine Mercy and Our Lady that make up the charism of my religious congregation, the Marian Fathers of the Immaculate Conception, so we are in the heart of the battle with you. Jesus told St. Faustina:

Tell My priests that hardened sinners will repent on hearing their words, meaning the priests when they speak about My unfathomable mercy, about the compassion I have for them in My Heart. To priests who proclaim and extol My mercy, I will give wondrous power; I will anoint their words and touch the hearts of those to whom they will speak (*Diary*, 1521).

Please pray that your priests faithfully live their promises and vows. Saint Faustina offers this beautiful prayer:

O my Jesus, I beg You on behalf of the whole Church: Grant it love and the light of Your Spirit, and give power to the words of priests so that hardened hearts might be brought to repentance and return to You, O Lord. Lord, give us holy priests; You yourself maintain them in holiness. O Divine and Great High Priest, may the power of Your mercy accompany them everywhere and protect them from the devil's traps and snares which are continually being set for the souls of priests. May the power of Your mercy, O Lord, shatter and bring to naught all that might tarnish the sanctity of priests, for You can do all things (*Diary*, 1052).

Saint John Vianney (1786-1859) is the patron saint of parish priests. Are you praying to him for good, holy priests? He drew the people back to the full practice of their Catholic faith with beauty: He decorated the church, used fine vessels, beautiful vestments, and so on to be appealing. He said we must give God the best of everything, which included himself. "My God," he implored, "grant me the conversion of my parish; I am willing to suffer all my life whatsoever it may please you to lay upon me; yes, even for 100 years I am prepared to endure the sharpest pains, only let my people be converted."[66] Thus, during his 44 years as a priest St. John Vianney was a true man of God as a great example for the people. We need priests like that today, with everything rocking the Church. Even so, Jesus loves His priests — always calling them to repentance. Like Christ, the Church is both human and divine. In her human nature, she will fail; but in her divine nature, she will never mislead. Please pray for holy priests.

Matrimony

> The matrimonial covenant, by which a man and a woman establish between themselves a partnership of the whole of life, is by its nature ordered toward the good of the spouses and the procreation and education of offspring; this covenant between baptized persons has been raised by Christ the Lord to the dignity of a sacrament.
>
> — *Catechism of the Catholic Church*, 1601

The family is the foundation of civilization, the bedrock of society. It not only allows humanity to exist through the centuries, it also allows mankind to share a special kind of love that imitates the Trinity. And as you know, the family begins with marriage. However, marriage is under attack today, as many governments, politicians, and special-interest groups are trying to redefine it, totally ignoring how God established it.

Sacramental marriage is one of the three major vocations; the others are the consecrated religious life and the single life (arguably). Marriage is a covenant between a man and a woman that establishes a partnership for life. It is a complete self-giving to the other, a total commitment in love. It is supernatural because God created man in His image as "male and female" (Gen 1:27) and the two become one flesh, as Jesus told the Pharisees:

> But from the beginning of creation, "God made them male and female." "For this reason a man

shall leave his father and mother and be joined to his wife, and the two shall become one flesh." So they are no longer two, but one flesh. Therefore what God has joined together, let no one separate (Mk 10:6-9).

This is what marriage is, a total commitment in love, where love is defined as "willing the good of the other," to give yourself completely to the other, even to death. That is why birth control, for example, is not love, as it is not completely giving oneself to the other. It is holding something back of yourself from the other; it becomes focused on self-pleasure. It can be like saying to your spouse, "I love you but not enough to have another one like you in the world. It will change my life, cut my free time, cost me money." We often put our emotions ahead of what true love is supposed to be.

Remember, love is not just an emotion — if it were, no marriage would ever last because emotions go up and down like an earthquake on the Richter scale. Love, rather, is an act of the will, a decision to love someone no matter what: I "choose" to love you always, no matter what happens, for better or for worse. Maybe that is why so many marriages are ending in divorce today, because we simply go by emotions without the commitment to stay the course. As I always say, nobody ever "feels" like getting up at 3 a.m. to change their child's dirty diaper, but parents do it because they love their baby. They make the decision to care for the child, they make an act of the will, although they don't necessarily always have giddy emotions while doing so. But in the end, they fulfill God's plan of giving love to the child.

That is why marriage is so important. In a special way, it is a complete giving (and receiving) of love, like the love found within the Trinity. In fact, St. Augustine shows us an amazing example.[67] He pointed out that God has to be a Trinity. Why? Because the one word that best describes God is "love." And in order to have love, you must have a community of persons. If I am the only person who ever existed and nobody else did, there could not be love. So, in the Trinity, we have love within a community of persons; it is all about relation and their love for one another.

In the source of love itself, the Godhead, God the Father is the lover; God the Son is the Beloved; and the Love between them is so great that from it proceeds a third person, the Holy Spirit. That is Who the Holy Spirit is, simply the love between the Father and the Son. And from that we see the family as a mirror of the Trinity. The father (husband) is the lover, the mother (wife) is the beloved, and the love between them is so great that from it proceeds a third person: the child. This is why marriage is between one man and one woman — this blessing of God in the gift of a child is not possible between two men or between two women.[68] Although two men can love each other and two women can love each other in a filial way, their love cannot be based in marriage. It is simply not God's design of nature, so who are we to try to redefine it? Contrary to what society has tried to do for the very first time in human history, we cannot redesign God's design of marriage.

"Marriage is a great Sacrament," St. Francis de Sales declared. "It is the nursery of Christianity, which fills the earth with true believers, to fill up the elect in Heaven. ... Would to God that his well-beloved Son were invited to all marriages, as he was to that of Cana. The wine of consolations and blessings would then never be wanting."[69] As a Sacrament, marriage gives a man and a woman the supernatural strength necessary to fight the good fight. Every victory achieved together over habit, routine, or boredom cements the bonds existing between the spouses and makes their love produce good fruit — literally.

Form, Matter, Minister

The *form* of a Catholic wedding is the consent given by the bride and groom, and the *matter* is the exchange of that consent (the recited vows from one spouse to the other). But as a precondition, a number of elements must come together for the Sacrament of Matrimony to occur. These are discussed with the engaged couple during the required premarital process (such as Pre-Cana) between them and the priest (the *minister*):

> **First,** a bride or groom who is a baptized Catholic must exchange marital vows before a priest or deacon in a Catholic church, or have received dispensation from the relevant Church authority to marry elsewhere. This means the marriage must have proper "canonical form." (Note: This does *not* apply to non-Catholics.)
>
> **Second,** the couple must freely and knowingly choose to enter the marriage. No so-called "shotgun weddings" or marriages solely for the purpose of gaining citizenship, for example, because neither is considered free consent.
>
> **Third,** the couple must understand what marriage is: a lifelong relationship open to children. My aunt married a man who said to her from the very beginning, "I absolutely refuse to have children." Later, she regretted the marriage because she wanted children. That is grounds for a marriage to be declared invalid because both parties were not open to life at the time they were (allegedly) married.
>
> **Fourth,** the couple must intend fidelity — to remain faithful to one another and faithful to God, 'til death do they part.

Fifth, they also must will the good of the other. For example, if someone marries another simply to be their sex outlet, that would not have the grounds for a valid sacramental marriage.

Sixth, they also must have the physical and psychological ability to follow through with their intentions.

Seventh, the marriage must be consummated — that is, the spouses must successfully complete the marital act. That is why any known impotence at the time of marriage is problematic for the validity of the marriage. If a sacramental marriage has been performed but has never been consummated, it's grounds for an annulment. Moreover, performing the marital act is not just about the formality of "checking the box" for a marriage to be valid. Much grace is offered to those who regularly renew the marital covenant on the marriage bed.

So, if any one (or more) of these conditions was not present at the time of a wedding, the marriage is not *sacramental*, meaning it is not valid in the eyes of the Catholic Church and to God based on Christ's words in Scripture. In these cases, the persons may pursue an annulment (a declaration of nullity) stating the marriage was not valid at the time the vows were exchanged, meaning the individuals are now free to remarry another person in the Catholic Church. It is not the dissolving of an existing marriage but rather a determination that something essential was lacking in what had been presumed to be a sacramental marital bond. Consent can also be lacking due to factors such as simulation (to pretend) or deceit (you were lied to).

Remember, an annulment is not a "Catholic divorce." It means that while there was a legal marriage, there was never a *sacramental* marriage in the first place. I should note, however, that many people fail to seek an annulment because they don't want their children to then be labeled as "illegitimate." This is not the case! Because they had a legal civil marriage — and in most cases, the couple even believed at the time of marriage that it was also a sacramental marriage — children from marriages that are later annulled are *not* illegitimate.

So, to conclude, when all of these above factors are properly brought together, you have a valid marriage — a sacramental, indissoluble union that no human can dissolve.

How is marriage entered into? This is where it gets very interesting. The husband and the wife enter into vows with each other, which are greater than promises. Vows involve greater accountability and sacredness than promises. I might promise to cook you dinner every single night but sometimes a circumstance may arise that causes me to have to break that promise. "Sorry, I can't cook dinner tonight." But if I vow before God and others that I will love and honor you all the days of my life — which is basically what you do at a wedding — circumstances should *never* cause me to break that vow, no matter what. God and the community hold me to a greater accountability.

Almost all cultures treat vows as sacred as compared to everyday promises. Vows are a mirror of God's promises to us through His covenants, sending Jesus Christ His Son to Earth through the Gospel and the institution of the Church. God freely and deliberately committed to us, so our vows to each other mirror that. This is why a wedding ring should always be worn and why it should have deep meaning for you as a visible sign of your vows.

Catholic marriage vows are based on a declaration of consent. The priest asks three questions: "[Name] and [name], have you come here to enter into marriage without coercion, freely and wholeheartedly?" "Are you prepared, as you follow the path of marriage, to love and honor each other for as long as you both shall live?" "Are you prepared to accept children lovingly from God and to bring them up according to the law of Christ and His Church?" They answer to each, "I am." But before you answer this for yourself, I suggest you put much time and prayer into discernment of this monumental step, asking God for His guidance in your life.

Three Objectives of Marriage

The three objectives of a sacramental marriage are union, procreation, and the salvation of your spouse. I tell all the couples I prepare for marriage that I see two things present in every marriage that is flourishing, yet lacking in every marriage that is failing: prayer and the conjugal act. The union of the spouses in the marital act allows for the other objectives of procreation (children result from the unimpeded marital act) and getting your spouse to Heaven (the union of the marital act begets bonding and communication, which are necessary for true love to flourish, and love gets us to Heaven). Getting your spouse to Heaven is the ultimate love. There's no greater good.

Consider what Dietrich von Hildebrand (a great philosopher and one of my favorite writers) and his wife, Alice, wrote about the true meaning of love:

> A person truly in love wants to bind himself forever to his beloved — which is precisely the gift that marriage gives him. In contrast, love without an unqualified commitment betrays the very essence of love. He who refuses to commit himself (or who breaks a commitment in order to start another relationship) fools himself. He confuses the excitement of novelty with authentic happiness. Such affective defeatism — so typical of our age — is a symptom or a severe emotional immaturity which weakens the very foundation of society. It is rooted partly in a misunderstanding of freedom. Many people criticize marriage because

they fail to realize that a person also exercises his freedom when he freely binds himself to another in marriage. ... Marriage calls each spouse to fight against himself for the sake of his beloved. This is why it has become so unpopular today. People are no longer willing to achieve the greatest of all victories, the victory over self.[70]

We said marriage is a total commitment in love, so let's now expand on love. It is a complete giving *and* receiving, just as the marital act is supposed to be. Many marriages fail because there's no giving, no receiving, or both. We need both reciprocal giving and receiving in love for marriage to work. It's like the love within the Trinity, which is complete giving and receiving. When spouses conceive new life, they participate in God's creative power. Union of the spouses makes the husband and the wife become one flesh: "Therefore a man leaves his father and his mother and clings to his wife, and they become one flesh" (Gen 2:24).

The act of complete giving and receiving is a good way to explain again why contraception is not allowed by the Church. Earlier we mentioned that contraception is wrong because it puts a barrier between the complete giving and receiving of love in the marital act. It's as if one spouse says to the other, "I can't let you be intimate with me because we just can't have another child right now." The Church, in her compassion, understands that methods like Natural Family Planning can address those concerns by simultaneously allowing the marriage to be fully expressed between the man and the woman (fully giving to each other), yet to potentially not have a child every time the marital act is enjoyed.

This is important, because I have observed in my own marriage counseling of couples who came to me with problems and irreconcilable differences, that 100 percent of them were not engaging in the marital act. On the contrary, of the couples I've spoken to who were flourishing and finding fulfillment in one another, 100 percent of them were engaging in the marital act.

Women Do *What?*

Marriage is a covenant between a man and a woman that establishes a partnership for life. But what about that famous Bible passage that strikes fear into every priest for his Sunday homily? Yes, when St. Paul tells wives to be *subordinate* (submissive) to their husbands. How can the submission of one simultaneously allow for equality with the other? It is perhaps one of the most misunderstood passages in the entire Bible. Let's reread the passage from the Letter to the Ephesians:

> Be subordinate to one another out of reverence for Christ. Wives should be subordinate to their husbands as to the Lord. For the husband is head of his wife just as Christ is head of the church, he himself the savior of the body. As the church is subordinate to Christ, so wives should be subordinate to their husbands in everything. Husbands, love your wives, even as Christ loved the church and handed himself over for her to sanctify her, cleansing her by the bath of water with the word, that he might present to himself the church in splendor, without spot or wrinkle or any such thing, that she might be holy and without blemish. So [also] husbands should love their wives as their own bodies. He who loves his wife loves himself. For no one hates his own flesh but rather nourishes and cherishes it, even as Christ does the church, because we are members of his body. "For this reason a man shall leave [his] father and [his] mother and be joined to his wife, and the two shall become one flesh." This

is a great mystery, but I speak in reference to Christ and the church. In any case, each one of you should love his wife as himself, and the wife should respect her husband (Eph 5:21-33).[71]

So, what does St. Paul mean when he says wives should be subordinate/submissive to their husbands? It's not what you may think.

Let's look at husbands first. Husbands, St. Paul is saying, love your wives, even to the point of death, as Christ loved the Church and handed Himself over for her. Headship of the husband in a marriage is not about worldly power or degradation of the wife. The Greek word for "head" is *kephale*, which doesn't mean "boss." It means "one who brings fulfillment to." This is the same word used to describe Christ as Head of the Church, which is His Body. The head and the body are one, like the unity of husband and wife. They depend on each other for fullness.

Now men, be careful here because you are not to exploit this passage. I remember my dad used to elbow my mom in church when they would read, "Wives, be submissive to your husbands." But a complete reading shows they are to be subject to each other, just in different ways. A wife subjects herself to her husband by accepting his role as the head. That means that she cooperates with him in filling that role of service to her and her children. Now the husband, in return, subjects himself first to God, and then his wife, by accepting her need for love and to care for her to the point that he would give his life. The Church teaches this is mutual subjection; it's not about domination. God created both male and female, so they have different but complementary and equal roles.

My favorite television programs before I became a priest were *Everybody Loves Raymond*, *Home Improvement*, *Married with Children*, *The Simpsons*, and *King of Queens*. It wasn't until later that I realized what all these shows had in common: They're making a buffoon out of the husband and father. He's an idiot. The father isn't the leader, he's not the head — the wife is. She is the only competent person in the marriage. It makes one wonder about what agenda Hollywood had back then and still has. As a result, this is the way society today wants to destroy the nuclear family, the patriarchy, the way God set it up. Who are we to destroy what God established? This leads to chaos. Even Jesus followed the rules of the family given by God. Jesus was the most important member of the Holy Family, followed by Mary. But who was the head? It was Joseph.

Contrary to what our culture tells us, the Catholic Church is not anti-woman — far from it. Pope St. John Paul II said that authentic love requires that a man have profound respect for the equal dignity of his wife. He cited St. Ambrose: "You are not her lord, but her husband. She is not your slave, but your wife. ... Reciprocate her attentiveness to you and be grateful to her for her love."[72] In his 1930 encyclical *Casti Connubii*, Pope Pius XI wrote:

> For if the man is the head, the woman is the heart, and as he occupies the chief place in ruling, so she may and ought to claim for herself the chief place in love. Again, this subjection of wife to husband in its degree and manner may vary according to the different conditions of persons, place and time. In fact, if the husband neglects his duty, it falls to the wife to take his place in directing the family. But the structure of the family and its fundamental law, established and confirmed by God, must always and everywhere be maintained intact.[73]

If a husband is not a husband who lays down his life for his bride and puts her ahead of himself, he has no business pointing to that Ephesians passage by saying, "Be subordinate to me." When wives are told to be subject to their husbands, it has nothing to do with status. Two persons can be equal in status, while one is subordinate to the other. Look at the Trinity, where the Father, Son, and Holy Spirit are equal but the Son subordinates Himself to the Father, and the Holy Spirit is subordinated to the Son. That doesn't mean Jesus or the Holy Spirit is inferior. All three are equal.

"Sub" means "under," so submission means putting yourself *under* your husband's *mission*, which is to get you and your children to Heaven. So, wives, please give your husbands a chance as leader of the family. If your husband fails, then you may have to take over. And may the grace of Almighty God and the Holy Spirit help you in that endeavor.

A good analogy here is one I heard years ago: ballroom dancing. Both husband and wife are subject to Christ, just like the man and woman are subject to the music of the dance. A woman cannot submit, however, if the leading man is stepping all over her toes during the dance. It's the same in marriage: a woman cannot submit to an abusive husband who is not following the music of God. In the same way, the man can't lead if the wife tries to push him all over the dance floor. In a marriage, the husband can't lead the family with a perpetually domineering or nagging wife. Both, therefore, need to let the Holy Spirit lead them in faith, or there can be no dance and certainly no marriage. If you choose marriage (like a dance), the husband accepts the duty to lead and the wife to follow, again in an equal and dignified way.

Divorce

Marriage has become very misunderstood in today's secular culture. Gay "marriage" is more and more common, and the divorce rate is rising. Remember what Sr. Lucia, the eldest Fatima visionary, said about the final battle between God and Satan? "The decisive battle between the kingdom of Christ and Satan will be over marriage and the family. And those who will work for the good of the family will experience persecution and tribulation. But do not be afraid, because Our Lady has already crushed his head."[74]

So, what is the Catholic Church's teaching on divorce? Christ opens the door for us here in Matthew's Gospel, Canon law, and the *Catechism of the Catholic Church*, which present His teachings in their essence:

> Some Pharisees approached [Jesus], and tested him, saying, "Is it lawful for a man to divorce his wife for any cause whatever?" He said in reply, "Have you not read that from the beginning the Creator 'made them male and female' and said, 'For this reason a man shall leave his father and mother and be joined to his wife, and the two shall become one flesh'? So they are no longer two, but one flesh. Therefore, what God has joined together, no human being must separate." They said to him, "Then why did Moses command that the man give the woman a bill of divorce and dismiss [her]?" He said to them, "Because of the hardness of your hearts Moses allowed you to divorce your wives, but from the beginning it was not so. I say to you, whoever divorces his wife (unless the marriage is unlawful) and marries another commits adultery." [His] disciples said to him, "If that is the case of a man with his wife, it is better not to marry." He answered, "Not all can accept [this] word, but only those to whom that is granted. Some are incapable of marriage because they were born so; some, because they were made so by others; some, because they have renounced marriage for the sake of the kingdom of heaven. Whoever can accept this ought to accept it" (Mt 19:3-12; see also Mk 10:2-12).[75]

Basically, the reason Moses allowed divorce was concession, because if the husband was not going to take care of his wife, he should let go of his right to her. I'm not intending to speak here as if she's property. This is just the way it was in first-century Palestine at the time of Christ and back earlier to Moses. This allowed another man to marry her and to provide for her. Jesus showed that the form of divorce Moses granted was not part of God's original plan, but was allowed because of the stubbornness of the husband who wasn't taking care of his wife. So, Jesus is basically saying that divorce is only tolerated based on man's hardness of heart. In fact, the Greek word *apoluo*, translated *divorce*, means relinquishment of a legal right.

Now, if you are baptized, a sacramental marriage is indissoluble and nobody can cancel that bond, not even the Church. Civil divorce affects marriage legally, but not the Sacrament. The Church doesn't involve itself in the legal aspect of marriage, but it does so in moral law, and that's what the Sacrament of Matrimony is about.

So, can divorce ever be allowed? Canon law says it is best first to try to get permission from your local bishop for a separation (see 1151-1155). That's the recommended first step: talk to your parish priest about how to do that. Of course, in a real emergency, if your or your children's safety is in danger, leaving your house for a safe place is permissible and even encouraged. The *Catechism* says if this separation doesn't resolve the issues in your marriage, then a civil divorce may be permitted. But under ordinary circumstances, is it a sin? The *Catechism* states,

> Divorce is a grave offense against the natural law. ... Divorce does injury to the covenant of salvation, of which sacramental marriage is the sign. Contracting a new union, even if it is recognized by civil law, adds to the gravity of the rupture: the remarried spouse is then in a situation of public and permanent adultery. ... Divorce is immoral also because it introduces disorder into the family and into society (2384-2385).

This is why Christ said, "Therefore what God has joined together, let no one separate" (Mt 19:6). Based on this verse and the *Catechism*, we can surmise that a civil divorce *may be* sinful in and of itself. I'll repeat that: *may be* sinful. Why "may be" and not "is"? Because one spouse may be innocent, such as being abandoned. For instance, a family member of mine was married for 24 years when her husband left her, declaring he didn't feel the "fireworks" anymore when he gazed into her eyes. I believe she was innocent because she didn't want the divorce even though she signed the divorce papers, because her husband abandoned her for a bad reason. How can I say it's a bad reason? If people aren't in love anymore, isn't that a valid reason for a divorce? The answer is no.

Let's return to the very important point that love is not just an emotion but an act of the will. If every married couple based their marriage solely on emotion, we'd likely see even more astronomical divorce rates than we see already, because emotions change every day. We have good days and we have bad days, obviously. The choice to love your spouse, to will good for them, is your responsibility once you make those vows, even if you go through a range of emotions and feelings. If we neglect this teaching and simply run to divorce court, divorce *may be* sinful.

However, the *Catechism* also says, "It can happen that one of the spouses is the innocent victim of a divorce decreed by civil law; this spouse therefore has not contravened the moral law" (2386). That means they are not guilty of sin. The *Catechism* goes on to say, "There is a considerable difference between a spouse who has sincerely tried to be faithful to the Sacrament of Marriage and is unjustly abandoned, and one who through his own grave fault destroys a canonically valid marriage."

The *Catechism* further explains, "If civil divorce remains the only possible way of ensuring certain legal rights, the care of the children, or the protection of inheritance, it can be tolerated and doesn't constitute a moral offense" (2383).

In Canon law, we find even more information: "If either of the spouses causes grave mental or physical danger to the other spouse or to the offspring or otherwise renders common life too difficult, that spouse gives the other a legitimate cause for leaving" (1153). As such, divorce is not necessarily a sin, but remarriage without an annulment is a sin.

In some translations, Jesus says that a marriage cannot be dissolved, "except for unchastity." Actually, that doesn't mean that any slip of fidelity from your spouse constitutes an invalid marriage. "Unchastity" as used in this case means "invalid marriage," not adultery. That is why the better translation is "unlawfulness," which means the marriage didn't follow the legal requirements for a valid marriage from the outset. In such cases, there are grounds for an annulment.

Is Your Marriage Valid? Annulments

What option does someone have in a case where the marriage is unlawful? One may seek an annulment. In Scripture, Jesus says, "I say to you, whoever divorces his wife (unless the marriage is unlawful) and marries another commits adultery" (Mt 5:32).[76] The key word here is "unlawful." The Church says that if a marriage doesn't follow the requirements for a valid sacramental marriage, as previously listed, it can be annulled. As mentioned, annulment is not a Catholic divorce but rather an official declaration that one, some, or all of the requirements for a valid sacramental marriage were not present at the time of the wedding ceremony, or there was an impediment (more on that to come) that meant one or both of the persons should never have entered into the marriage.

An annulment also acknowledges that, until the annulment is handed down and official, a marriage was believed to be present, so any children from that union are not illegitimate. This point is often misunderstood and a hindrance to people trying to follow Church law. If you are divorced, have not received an annulment, and have not remarried civilly, the Church regards your sacramental marriage as still valid. Therefore, you may receive Holy Communion, as long as you are in the state of grace. You may not receive Holy Communion if you have civilly remarried without an annulment, as in the eyes of the Church you are committing adultery because you are still sacramentally married. A rule of thumb is that divorce is not necessarily a sin, but remarriage without an annulment is *always* a sin.

If you have been divorced, or are contemplating divorce, or if there's anything in your marital history that's impeding you from receiving the Sacraments of the Church, it's not too late to put yourself right with Church law. If you need to have a marriage annulled or *convalidated* — which means a marriage outside of the Church can later get a blessing as long as neither person was married before — it's not too late to straighten out your situation. Go to your priest. The process in the past has been long and complicated, involving the tribunal of your diocese, but this is now changing and becoming less arduous. Honestly, this matter is of such importance that no amount of time or effort should dissuade you from following Christ's command. Sparing inconvenience is not a reason to put your soul in jeopardy.

The Catholic Church recognizes two types of marriage: *sacramental* and *natural*. The marriage is sacramental if both spouses are baptized Christians, even non-Catholic, as long as there are no impediments for either spouse to enter into marriage. Surprisingly, even if both spouses are not Catholic, as long as they are baptized Christians with no impediments, they have a sacramental marriage. It all depends on the Baptism of the spouses. This kind of marriage cannot receive a divorce (let no man separate what God has joined). Even civil divorce does not affect the sacramental nature of marriage, so it's still valid.

If either spouse is unbaptized, the marriage is valid if there are no impediments, but rather than being a sacramental marriage, it is a "natural marriage," meaning a valid marriage based on the natural law and human consent. The marriage, however, lacks grace through Baptism. Here the Church recognizes the marriage of unbaptized non-Catholics as valid marriages in an earthly sense, as long as there are no impediments. A natural marriage can be dissolved in certain circumstances. Finally, if non-baptized persons are later baptized, the marriage goes from natural to sacramental.

So, if you or your future spouse are divorced from a sacramental marriage and wish to remarry (even for a Catholic marrying a non-Catholic), you or that future spouse must first obtain an annulment and then remarry in the Catholic Church. I found this out first-hand when I was engaged in North Carolina to a young woman who had been married prior to my meeting her. I thought, *Well, she wasn't married in the Catholic Church, so I don't need an annulment.* However, she was baptized and married in the Baptist Church, so the Catholic Church recognizes this union. If you have two validly baptized people who get married and don't have any conditions as we listed earlier — for example, being in an arranged marriage — the marriage is sacramental, even if it's not in the Catholic Church. Again, everything is determined by Baptism.

Now, we've mentioned the word "impediment" several times. *What are impediments to getting married?* Sometimes a person enters into marriage with full consent and proper form, but something in their background makes marriage not possible. These circumstances can include:

- One or both parties is below the minimum age of 16 for males and 14 for females.
- Impotence (not sterility).
- Being already married.
- One person is Catholic and the other hasn't been baptized (unless permitted).

- The man was ordained to the priesthood.
- Either party made a public perpetual vow of chastity in a religious order.
- Conviction of a crime such as bringing about the death of one's spouse, or the spouse of another, with the intention of marriage.
- Consanguinity, or close relationship by blood (incest).
- Affinity, or close relationship by marriage.[77]

We all recognize that marriage takes perseverance and is not easy, but the rewards are great. Please talk to your priest. He is there to help and answer your questions. Please make things right with the Church and thus with your soul.

Some Interesting Final Points

We finish with a few interesting facts. Approximately 94 percent of petitions for annulments filed in the United States are granted. The United States has only 6 percent of the world's Catholics, but 60 percent of the annulments granted worldwide are in the United States. Twenty-seven thousand marriages were declared null in this country in 2007, compared to just 338 in 1968.[78] In addition, the divorce rate in the United States is about 50 percent, and the Catholic rate is about the same. This is due to many factors in the West, including cultural shifts, children who have only one parent, embracing promiscuous morals, and most of all increasing numbers of people not practicing their faith.

Perhaps here in the West, we can learn from my relatives in the East. In Široki-Brijeg, Bosnia, which is all Croatian Catholic, there has never been a recorded divorce in more than 26,000 marriages. In their wedding ceremony, the priest blesses the crucifix presented by the bride and groom. He places the bride's right hand upon the crucifix, then that of the groom upon hers, and covers them with a stole. The couple then makes their vows with their hands clasping the crucifix. The priest tells them they have found the ideal "partner," with whom they must share their lives, with the following words: "You have found your cross! It is a cross that you must love and take with you every day of your lives. Know how to appreciate it." They kiss it, then put it in their home, showing their belief that a family must be born of the cross. Wow.

~ AFTERWORD ~
Outside the Church, There is No Salvation

If you've reached this point, you should have a good understanding of the fact that the Sacraments are God's gift to us, the quickest way to Heaven. The Sacraments are unique to the Catholic Church, East and West, the "Petrine" Church founded by Jesus Christ Himself. Other Christian churches have some valid sacraments, but only the Catholic Church has the fullness of the truth, including all seven Sacraments, full communion with the successor to St. Peter, and perhaps most importantly, the Most Holy Eucharist.

You may have heard the expression *Extra Ecclesiam nulla salus*, which means, "Outside the Church, there is no salvation." Is this true? The Church has always taught that it is. The Fourth Lateran Council in 1215 stated, "There is indeed one universal church of the faithful, outside of which nobody at all is saved, in which Jesus Christ is both priest and sacrifice."[79] Blessed Pope Pius IX declared in 1863:

> It is again necessary to mention and censure a very grave error entrapping some Catholics who believe that it is possible to arrive at eternal salvation although living in error and alienated from the true faith and Catholic unity. Such belief is certainly opposed to Catholic teaching. ... Also well-known is the Catholic teaching that no one can be saved outside the Catholic Church. Eternal salvation cannot be obtained by those who oppose the authority and statements of the same Church and are stubbornly separated from the unity of the Church and also from the successor of Peter, the Roman Pontiff, to whom "the custody of the vineyard has been committed by the Savior."[80]

But I am asked all the time, "Father, what about my non-Catholic friends and my family? They're great people; they will certainly be in Heaven!" And then there's this: "Father, Vatican II declared that non-Catholics can be saved. What's that all about?" So how do we understand this? Well, let's talk this through.

Some people go to one extreme, claiming that it makes no difference if you are Catholic or not in order to be saved. They exclaim it doesn't matter what you are or what you believe or what religion you profess, because God doesn't care. The other extreme says, unless you are a baptized, card-carrying, registered member of the Roman Catholic Church sitting in the pew every Sunday and receiving all the Sacraments, you're damned. Unless you're all in, you'll be all out.

Actually, both sides are wrong. The Church has rejected both of those extremes. Remember the Jesuit priest Fr. Leonard Feeney? He was actually excommunicated in 1949 by Ven. Pope Pius XII because he taught you *must* be a registered member of the Catholic Church in order to be saved. The Church condemned that attitude, which had become a big issue in the 1940s and 1950s. The Church made it clear that non-Catholics can get to Heaven (albeit on a much more difficult road), and also drove home the key point that not all Catholics are guaranteed Heaven either.

Here's the crux of the issue: There is no salvation outside of Jesus. "All salvation comes from Christ the Head through the Church which is his Body," according to the *Catechism* (846). It proceeds to quote essential passages from *Lumen Gentium*, the Dogmatic Constitution on the Church from the Second Vatican Council. First, it addressed the necessity of the Church for salvation:

> This Sacred Council wishes to turn its attention firstly to the Catholic faithful. Basing itself upon Sacred Scripture and Tradition, it teaches that the

Church, now sojourning on earth as an exile, is necessary for salvation. Christ, present to us in His Body, which is the Church, is the one Mediator and the unique way of salvation. In explicit terms He Himself affirmed the necessity of faith and baptism (see Mk 16:16; Jn 3.5) and thereby affirmed also the necessity of the Church, for through baptism as through a door men enter the Church (*Lumen Gentium*, 14).

The Council added that anyone who, "knowing that the Catholic Church was made necessary by Christ, would refuse to enter or to remain in it, could not be saved."

The Council Fathers also recognized "those who, being baptized, are honored with the name of Christian," but are not in communion with the Catholic Church. In this case, the prayer is for unity:

> We can say that in some real way they are joined with us in the Holy Spirit, for to them too He gives His gifts and graces whereby He is operative among them with His sanctifying power. Some indeed He has strengthened to the extent of the shedding of their blood. In all of Christ's disciples the Spirit arouses the desire to be peacefully united, in the manner determined by Christ, as one flock under one shepherd, and He prompts them to pursue this end. Mother Church never ceases to pray, hope and work that this may come about. She exhorts her children to purification and renewal so that the sign of Christ may shine more brightly over the face of the earth. (*Lumen Gentium*, 15).

But what about non-Christians, those who innocently do not know God or the Church? The Council stated:

> Nor is God far distant from those who in shadows and images seek the unknown God, for it is He who gives to all men life and breath and all things, and as Savior wills that all men be saved. Those also can attain to salvation who through no fault of their own do not know the Gospel of Christ or His Church, yet sincerely seek God and moved by grace strive by their deeds to do His will as it is known to them through the dictates of conscience. Nor does Divine Providence deny the helps necessary for salvation to those who, without blame on their part, have not yet arrived at an explicit knowledge of God and with His grace strive to live a good life. Whatever good or truth is found amongst them is looked upon by the Church as a preparation for the Gospel (*Lumen Gentium*, 16).

So, there are exceptions, and we can see salvation for those outside of the physical four walls of the Catholic Church. However, it is much more difficult for them than for Catholics because of graces given through the Church, such as the Sacraments. Remember the workers who labored for different amounts of time but got the same pay? The Sacraments make our journey to Heaven much more straightforward — and expedited.

Well, then, what about Catholics who have left the Faith? Are they okay, or are they lost? It would be the height of presumption to say that someone who has left the Faith "is okay." Now, perhaps a person who left the Faith had such a distorted notion of what the Church truly is and what she teaches that there may not be full culpability.

However, it may well be that they are culpable, so no amount of church attendance or prayer apart from the Church that Jesus established, the Catholic Church, will get them to Heaven. So, we must take seriously anyone who has left the Faith or anyone who is not in union with the

Church because, objectively speaking (barring invincible ignorance, etc.), souls are on the line!

In the Bible, Who Can Be Saved?

The Bible tells us in absolute terms that the Church is needed for salvation. Look at John 14:6: "I am the way, and the truth, and the life. No one comes to the Father except through me." We all know this, and it's not only Christ Who is essential, but also Christ speaking through His Church as His Body. He's talking to the apostles, the first leaders of the Church, the first bishops of the Church, the first pope of the Church. Saint Paul writes in his Letter to the Ephesians, "through the church the wisdom of God in its rich variety might now be made known to the rulers and authorities in the heavenly places" (Eph 3:10).

Christ established the Catholic Church, and there was only one "Petrine" Catholic Church for 1,000 years, until the Great Schism occurred between West and East in 1054. Five hundred years later, the Protestant Reformation erupted. But does anybody think Jesus would come to Earth and say, "I'm going to start a Church" — which He did — but then say, "I'm going to get it wrong for 1,500 years until Martin Luther gets it right?" That's not possible. You can't just create your own religion and follow the Jesus of your own creation, the Jesus that some guy wants Him to be.

As I mentioned, some 45,000 Christian denominations are present around the world, and every single one was created by a man or woman, except the Catholic Church. No other Christian religion can claim they were started by Jesus Christ. The Catholic Church, West and East, is the only one started by Christ in the apostles, and the only one that is truly sacramental.

In the Catholic Church with the Sacraments, if you're in a state of grace and acting in love, you're confidently hopeful of your salvation. With all the other ways it's possible, but saving grace is not guaranteed. This is what Christ said: It's through the Church. You must be baptized and have your sins forgiven. Receive the Bread of Life that only comes to the churches with Apostolic Succession. There is no true Eucharist at the Protestant houses of worship because it's not sacramental transubstantiation, the true Body of Christ. Even they admit to that.

Some Protestant churches actually have the Sacraments of Baptism and Marriage, so they can be in some form of relationship with the Catholic Church. They're not formally registered, but they have a link to our Church. They share some of the truth that our religion holds, that Jesus is our Savior, He died for our sins, and Scripture is the inerrant Word of God. So, if folks outside of the visible boundaries of the Catholic Church are truly seeking the truth and have not rejected the fullness of the truth found in the Catholic Church, they have the possibility of being saved.

Theologian Jimmy Akin said, "If they are genuinely committed to seeking the truth, then they are implicitly committed to seeking Jesus and living by His commands; they just don't *know* that He is the Truth they're seeking (see John 14:6)."[81] Thus the Church can serve as the sacrament of salvation even for those outside her visible borders. But if they had full knowledge and freedom in their rejection of full communion with the Catholic Church, their soul is lost — but only God knows. Also keep in mind that we who have been given the gift of the Catholic faith have an obligation to bring others to it.

Ignorance and Knowledge

Ignorance is *not* bliss. It's dangerous. If non-Catholics are ignorant of the truth through no fault of their own, then the limited amount of truth that they do have serves as a preparation for when God reveals Himself to them at some point, maybe even at the moment of their death. According to the *Catechism*:

> The Catholic Church recognizes in other religions that search, among shadows and images, for the God who is unknown yet near since he gives life and breath and all things and wants all men to be saved. Thus, the Church considers all goodness and truth found in these religions as "a preparation for the Gospel and given by him who enlightens all men that they may at length have life" (843).

There are elements of truth in other religions that can be a preparation for the Gospel, and if people live primarily in the light of those true elements, though invincibly ignorant of the fullness of the Catholic faith, then they have a bridge to saving grace, so to speak, and can possibly be saved. As we will see, "invincibly ignorant" does not mean just because a person is "ignorant" of the truth, they *will automatically* be saved. What it means is that they have *the possibility* of salvation, but if they are ignorant due to apathy or dislike for the faith, then this is not applicable.

Saint Justin Martyr (A.D. 100-165) held that those who had not heard the Gospel could be saved if they lived according to reason, and the Greek word he used is *logos*. This is the same word that St. John used to refer to the pre-incarnate and incarnate Christ. In the prologue of his Gospel, the idea was that without explicitly hearing Christ preached, some Gentiles lived according to reason, according to the laws of God, and thus had a kind of implicit connection with Christ that would enable them to be saved. It was still through Christ and His Church that they *would* be saved, though they didn't know that in this life. "From his fullness we have all received, grace upon grace. The law indeed was given through Moses; grace and truth came through Jesus Christ" (Jn 1:16-17).

So today the Church holds to both of these themes. It recognizes the necessity of Christ and His Church for salvation, but it also recognizes that some people who are not fully incorporated into His Church can still be related to it in a way that makes salvation possible for them, albeit difficult. The fact that it's possible for people to be saved without being fully incorporated into the Church, though, doesn't mean that they don't need to hear the message of Christ or that we don't need to evangelize them. After all, Jesus Himself said, "Go therefore, and make disciples of all nations, baptizing them in the name of the Father and of the Son and of the Holy Spirit" (Mt 28:19).

What About Non-Catholics and Non-Christians?

As a seminarian, I disagreed with the section of the *Catechism* on the Catholic Church's relationship with Muslims:

> The plan of salvation also includes those who acknowledge the Creator, in the first place amongst whom are the Muslims; these profess to hold the faith of Abraham, and together with us they adore the one, merciful God, mankind's judge on the last day (841).

This upset me. You mean Muslims worship the same God as us? That's impossible. Our God is Trinitarian; theirs is not. There is no Incarnation in their god. Their god would never condescend to become one of us sinful humans. They reject Jesus.

Well, I'm older and (hopefully) wiser now, and I can see where the *Catechism* is going with this. We are not fully responsible for ignorance of the Catholic faith. Neither a Muslim, nor a Jew, nor a Buddhist, nor any Protestant will be saved by being a "good" person. You are only saved because of Jesus Christ. If those people get to Heaven, it won't be because of their religion, but in spite of it. Other religions can help in some ways, but can also hinder salvation. It's about knowledge.

The Church's understanding, Jimmy Akin says, is that Muslims don't fully understand God, but that fact doesn't make them necessarily rotten or evil. They're good or bad based on their free-will choices, just like us. It doesn't mean that they aren't genuinely directing their prayers toward a true Creator. They just have some incomplete or erroneous understanding of Him. I like Jimmy's pop culture explanation:

> Suppose that you and I both knew millionaire Bruce Wayne. I might know, because he revealed it to me, that he is also Batman. You may hear this claim and reject it, in which case you adopt the false corollary belief "Batman is *not* Bruce Wayne." That does not mean that you don't know and relate to either Bruce or Batman, it means only that you misunderstand the relationship between them. In the same way, one may worship God and honor Jesus as a prophet (which He was) without understanding that Jesus *is* God. Indeed, many people in His own day did that: They knew the historical Jesus but had a false understanding of His identity.[82]

So, Muslims have errors, but they still have a genuine relationship with God, as do the Jews. Jews don't understand that God is a Trinity and they don't believe that Jesus is God. But that has never stopped the Church from recognizing that Jewish people worship God. If anyone is saved, it must in some sense be through the Church; in what sense, we can't say. There may be members of the Church whose membership is known to God alone.

So why be Catholic? The possibility of salvation for those who are not formally Catholic has led to the belief that all religions are equal. The Church condemns this false notion of equality among religions. Nobody who deliberately rejects the Truth in favor of something less than the fullness of Truth can be saved. Venerable Pope Pius XII made clear that others can be saved, but "they still remain deprived of those many heavenly gifts and helps which can only be enjoyed in the Catholic Church," and are, unfortunately, in a "state in which they cannot be sure of their salvation."[83] He said we must remember that we are not the judges of salvation; God is. We do not know who is "invincibly ignorant" and who isn't. Therefore, we must continue to "evangelize all men."

Thus, regarding who can be saved, as we have noted *Lumen Gentium* addresses Catholics, non-Christians, and non-Catholic Christians. Non-Christians, such as Pygmies in the rainforest, can be saved, but they will be judged different than us — they will be judged by the *natural law* and shown mercy because of their level of invincible ignorance. Non-Catholic Christians (like Protestants) will also be judged differently in that they will be judged by how well they followed Scripture, if they were baptized, etc. (their link to the Catholic Church). Finally, Catholics will be judged the harshest of all in one sense — Jesus said, "From everyone to whom much has been given, much will be required; and from the one to whom much has been entrusted, even more will be demanded" (Lk 12:48) — but not in another sense, because for them it will be the easiest because of the guaranteed grace in the Sacraments. We are judged on how we used the grace God gave us. But don't be afraid and say, "I don't want to be Catholic because too much is expected of me!" Actually, using the grace of God that saves us is easy — you just have to be open to it and seek to receive it. That's it.

I have explained it this way in the past: Three groups of people want to go from New York to Los Angeles. The non-Christians, like Jews and Muslims, can make the trip, but without any transportation tools, it would be like them walking the full distance from New York to LA. It's not impossible, but it will be very difficult, taking weeks (even months) to complete the journey.

Non-Catholic Christians, such as Protestants, have some tools, mainly Scripture and faith in Jesus Christ, even though they don't have full faith in His Church, so for them it would be like driving from New York to LA. Again, this is possible, but with the possibility of getting lost, running out of gas, or having a flat tire, it is also difficult, not to mention it will take several days to do it.

Then we have Catholics, who are given the fullness of the Truth. For them, going from New York to LA would be a breeze in their supersonic jet, only taking a few hours. It is like those who labored the least in the vineyard but got the same pay. They have the best tools available — the Sacraments — to get to their destination in the quickest, surest, and easiest way possible. So, your religion *does* matter!

That is why *Lumen Gentium* states that "the one Church of Christ ... *subsists* in the Catholic Church, governed by the Successor of Peter and by the Bishops in communion with him, although many elements of sanctification and truth can be found outside her structure. These elements, as gifts properly belonging to the Church of Christ, impel toward Catholic unity" (8).

How to Get to Heaven

I hear all the time, "Father, I'm a good person. I'll get to Heaven when I die." Or, "I'm fine; I never killed anybody." Well, Jesus' words in the Bible and the message conveyed to St. Faustina in her *Diary* say something a bit different. Narrow is the road to life and few follow it. Wide is the path to destruction and many are on it. Heaven is not a prize for those who are just good — it is for active disciples of Christ, since it is by grace alone that we are saved.

So, what does the Bible say we need to do to guarantee Heaven? Scripture lists five conditions for salvation: Baptism, Repentance (Confession), Faith, Keeping the Commandments (love), and the Eucharist. We can add prayer, because to do all of these we need a relationship with Christ, and that comes through prayer. If you follow this plan, you'll be in a state of grace and ultimately be united with God. Notice that only one of these five conditions is about being a good, loving person — and even to live out that one, as with all the others, we need the help of God's grace, which is *guaranteed only in the Sacraments.*

We are saved by grace, but we must cooperate with that grace, and that is not done with words only. The good news is that we have grace in the Sacraments through the Church, through the Body of Christ. That is the same as saying *there is no salvation outside the Church.* You'll also notice that three of these five conditions are Sacraments: Baptism, Reconciliation (Penance), and Holy Eucharist. That is why when Jesus spoke of salvation, He offered these three verses:

- The one who believes and is baptized will be saved (Mk 16:16) — *Baptism*
- Unless you repent, you will all perish as they did (Lk 13:3) — *Confession*
- Those who eat my flesh and drink my blood have eternal life, and I will raise them up on the last day (Jn 6:54) — *Eucharist*

So, Jesus associated salvation with Baptism, Confession, and the Eucharist. Catholics recognize that these Sacraments are administered through the Church, so rejecting salvation on the terms Christ offers it is rejecting salvation itself. Since the Sacraments are the ordinary means through which Christ offers the grace necessary for salvation, and the Catholic Church that Christ established is the ordinary minister of those Sacraments, it is appropriate to state that salvation comes through the Church. It may be explained this way: Catholics have direct access to salvation through the Sacraments and Christ's Body, the Church; others have indirect, but possible, access.

Afterword

The bottom line? Start accepting Christ now, so that when He comes to you at the end of your life, it will be easier to say, "Yes!" And the best way to begin is by understanding the vital role of the Sacraments in getting you to Heaven. In addition, enrich your life in this world with faith, hope, and love, through an intimate relationship with the Savior Himself. I promise, it will be the most important thing you have ever done in your life!

Yes, God may provide an extraordinary way to salvation, but the Church is the ordinary way to salvation — so why risk it? Go to church. No non-Catholic religions will get you to Heaven in and of themselves. There is no salvation outside the Catholic Church, but remember there are no guarantees within it either — unless we receive the Sacraments and die in a state of grace with having the essence of charity in our lives.

The Sacraments will not only change your life on this earth; they will *guarantee* you life after death in Heaven. Just remember to be open to that grace by remaining in a state of grace. Jesus will do the rest. God bless you.

About the Author

Father Chris Alar, MIC, entered the Congregation of Marian Fathers of the Immaculate Conception of the Blessed Virgin Mary, the religious community entrusted with spreading the message and devotion of Divine Mercy, in 2006. Prior to that time, he received a Bachelor of Science in industrial engineering and a Masters of Business Administration (MBA) from the University of Michigan. After working as an engineering manager at a large automotive supplier in Detroit, he began his own consulting firm in Charlotte, North Carolina, in 2000.

Answering the Lord's call, he attended Franciscan University of Steubenville in Ohio for his philosophy studies; the Dominican House of Studies in Washington, D.C., for his theology studies; and he earned his Masters of Divinity degree from Holy Apostles Seminary in Cromwell, Connecticut. He was ordained to the priesthood on May 31, 2014.

Father Chris offers the popular "Divine Mercy 101" and "Explaining the Faith" YouTube series of talks and is the author of two bestselling books from Marian Press, *After Suicide: There's Hope for Them and for You* (with Fr. Jason Lewis, MIC), and *Understanding Divine Mercy*. He is host of the EWTN show *Living Divine Mercy*, which airs on Thursdays, 10 p.m. EST.

From 2014-2024, Father Chris served as "Fr. Joseph, MIC," the director of the Association of Marian Helpers, and as publisher of Marian Press. In 2024 he was elected Provincial Superior of the Blessed Virgin Mary, Mother of Mercy Province of the Marian Fathers of the Immaculate Conception in the United States and Argentina.

Watch Fr. Chris' "Explaining the Faith" talks and the EWTN *Living Divine Mercy* show on **DivineMercyPlus.org** and on **YouTube (Divine Mercy)**.

Endnotes

[1] St. Thomas Aquinas, *Summa Theologiae* I-II, q. 27, art. 2.
[2] John Henry Cardinal Newman, *Apologia pro Vita Sua* (New York: Longmans, Green, & Co., 1904), p. 17.
[3] NABRE.
[4] Aquinas, *Summa Theologica*, 2378, 2436.
[5] St. John Henry Newman, *Parochial and Plain Sermons* V, Sermon 10, "Righteousness not of us, but in us": https://catholiclibrary.org/library/view?docId=/Contemporary-EN/XCT.094.html;chunk.id=00000245 .
[6] Pope Leo XIII, encyclical *Divinum Illud Munus*, May 9, 1897, 6.
[7] Pope Benedict XVI, apostolic exhortation *Sacramentum Caritatis*, Feb. 22, 2007, 6.
[8] St. Francis de Sales, "The Spiritual Conferences": https://hosted.desales.edu/files/salesian/PDF/SalesienTextsTheSacraments.pdf.
[9] NABRE.
[10] Pope Innocent III, letter *Debitum pastoralis officii* to Berthold, the Bishop of Metz, Aug. 28, 1206, quoted in Denziger, *Sources of Dogma*, 412.
[11] Fr. Chris Alar, MIC, *Understanding Divine Mercy* (Stockbridge, MA: Marian Press, 2021), available in print and eBook formats on ShopMercy.org.
[12] Dogmatic Constitution on the Church *Lumen Gentium* (Nov. 21, 1964), 36:3.
[13] NABRE.
[14] St. Irenaeus, *Against Heresies* 2:22:4.
[15] St. John Chrysostom, *Baptismal Catecheses in Augustine, Against Julian* 1:6:21.
[16] St. Augustine, *The Literal Interpretation of Genesis* 10:23:39.
[17] Aquinas, *Summa Theologica* III, q. 69, a. 6.
[18] *The Apostolic Tradition* 21:16 (A.D. 215).
[19] Quoted in *The Letters and Diaries of John Henry Newman*, Charles Stephen Dessain et al., eds. (Oxford: Clarendon Press, 1984), 6:80.
[20] *Rite of Confirmation*, 5.
[21] See "What Happened to Confirmation Names?" Catholic Answers: www.catholic.com/qa/what-happened-to-confirmation-names.
[22] *Lumen Gentium*, 14.
[23] Aquinas, *Summa Theologica* III, 72, 8, ad 2.
[24] Quoted in *Catechism of the Catholic Church*, 1405.
[25] At the Shrine of Lagiewniki in Poland on June 7, 1997, Pope St. John Paul II said, "There is nothing that man needs more than Divine Mercy — that love which is benevolent, which is compassionate, which raises man above his weakness to the infinite heights of the holiness of God." See www.TheDivineMercy.org/message/john-paul-ii/homilies/1997-06-07.
[26] St. Francis de Sales, *Introduction to the Devout Life*, Part 2, Ch. 20: https://ccel.org/ccel/desales/devout_life/devout_life.iv.xx.html.
[27] St. Maria Faustina Kowalska, *Divine Mercy in My Soul* (Stockbridge, MA: Marian Press, 1987), 1804. Hereafter *Diary*.

[28] See St. John Chrysostom, *Catecheses* 3:13-19.

[29] I explain this further in my book *Understanding Divine Mercy*, chapter 1.

[30] "The Eucharistic Miracles of the World": www.miracolieucaristici.org.

[31] See Ronald Rychlak, "Eucharistic Miracles: Evidence of the Real Presence," Catholic Answers, June 24, 2019: www.catholic.com/magazine/print-edition/eucharistic-miracles-evidence-of-the-real-presence-0.

[32] St. Justin Martyr, *First Apology* 66.

[33] See "Facts about the Shroud of Turin (Age, Dimensions, Blood Stains," Magis Center: www.magiscenter.com/blog/facts-about-shroud-turin; "4 Approved Eucharistic Miracles from the 21st Century," Magis Center: www.magiscenter.com/blog/approved-eucharistic-miracles-21st-century; and Rick Becker, "Eucharistic Miracles and the Divine Blood Type," *National Catholic Register* blog, May 17, 2018: www.ncregister.com/blog/eucharistic-miracles-and-the-divine-blood-type.

[34] *Lumen Gentium*, 7.

[35] Quoted in Becker.

[36] See "A Matter of Faith, a Matter of Fact," TheDivineMercy.org, Dec. 19, 2012: www.thedivinemercy.org/articles/matter-faith-matter-fact; and Sabrina Ferrisi, "Three Eucharistic Miracles: Which Cases Have Undergone the Most Extensive Scientific Analysis?" *National Catholic Register*, June 11, 2023: www.ncregister.com/features/three-eucharistic-miracles-which-cases-have-undergone-the-most-extensive-scientific-analysis.

[37] Scott Hahn, *The Lamb's Supper: The Mass as Heaven on Earth* (London: PRH Christian Publishing, 2002), p. 4.

[38] Ibid., p. 5.

[39] St. Thérèse of Lisieux, *The Story of a Soul*, chapter 4, "Chapter IV: First Communion And Confirmation": www.ccel.org/ccel/therese/autobio.xii.html.

[40] Edward Pentin, "Guide to '24 Hours for the Lord'; Padre Pio and the Confessional," *National Catholic Register*, March 3, 2016: www.ncregister.com/blog/guide-to-24-hours-for-the-lord-padre-pio-and-the-confessional.

[41] NABRE.

[42] *Catechism of the Catholic Church*, 1033.

[43] To learn more, see "Confession: The Sacrament of Reconciliation," The National Shrine of The Divine Mercy: www.ShrineOfDivineMercy.org/confession-sacrament-reconciliation.

[44] St. Peter Chrysologus, *Sermon 84*, 7.

[45] NABRE.

[46] See R. C. Sproul, *The Holiness of God*, pp. 128–129; quoted in https://worldlysaints.wordpress.com/2017/01/04/martin-luther-his-confessions-and-battle-against-sin/_ftn1.

[47] To learn more about the extraordinary graces available on Divine Mercy Sunday, visit www.TheDivineMercy.org/celebrate.

[48] See Jonah McKeown, "Reconciliation on the rise? Catholics coming back to confession, poll suggests," Catholic News Agency, Oct. 1, 2024: www.catholicnewsagency.com/news/259543/reconciliation-on-the-rise-catholics-coming-back-to-confession-poll-suggests.

Endnotes

[49] See Very Rev. Peter Stravinskas, "The Holy Spirit in the Sacraments," Catholic Education Resource Center. https://catholiceducation.org/en/culture/the-holy-spirit-in-the-sacraments.html.

[50] To learn more about the extraordinary graces available on Divine Mercy Sunday, visit www.TheDivineMercy.org/celebrate.

[51] NABRE.

[52] For more information on the value of suffering and why God allows it, please see my book co-authored with Fr. Jason Lewis, MIC, *After Suicide: There's Hope for Them and for You* (Stockbridge, MA: Marian Press, 2019), available in print and eBook formats at ShopMercy.org.

[53] Origen, *Homilies on Leviticus* 2:4.

[54] See the National Shrine of St. Maximilian Kolbe at Marytown website: https://kolbeshrine.org/about-saint-maximilian.

[55] According to Msgr. Stuart Swetland, quoted in Lindsey Kettner, "Can my non-Catholic friend receive Anointing of the Sick?" Relevant Radio, June 8, 2018: https://relevantradio.com/2018/06/can-my-non-catholic-friend-receive-anointing-of-the-sick/.

[56] See Fr. Charles Grondin, "The Apostolic Pardon," Catholic Answers: www.catholic.com/qa/the-apostolic-pardon.

[57] To learn more, see "Praying for the Sick and Dying": www.TheDivineMercy.org/eadm/praying. To learn how to pray the Chaplet of The Divine Mercy, visit www.TheDivineMercy.org/message/devotions/chaplet or download the Divine Mercy app on Apple, Amazon, and Google Play.

[58] Scott Hahn, *Kinship by Covenant: A Canonical Approach to the Fulfillment of God's Saving Promises* (New Haven, CT: Yale University Press, 2009), pp. 406-407; see also Tim Gray, "In the Order of Melchizedek," St. Paul Center for Biblical Theology, August 6, 2019: https://stpaulcenter.com/in-the-order-of-melchizedek/.

[59] There are a number of good sources for information and statistics: National Sexual Violence Resource Center, "Get Statistics": www.nsvrc.org/statistics; Philip Jenkins, "Myth of a Catholic Crisis," *The American Conservative*, June 1, 2010: www.theamericanconservative.com/articles/myth-of-a-catholic-crisis;. Jenkins, "Forum: The Myth of the 'Pedophile Priest'": *Pittsburgh Post-Gazette*, March 3, 2002, http://old.post-gazette.com/forum/comm/20020303edjenk03p6.asp; Pat Wingert, "Priests Commit No More Abuse Than Other Males," *Newsweek*, April 7, 2010: www.newsweek.com/priests-commit-no-more-abuse-other-males-70625; John Jay College of Criminal Justice, "The Nature and Scope of Sexual Abuse of Minors by Catholic Priests and Deacons in the United States 1950-2002," February 2004: www.usccb.org/issues-and-action/child-and-youth-protection/upload/The-Nature-and-Scope-of-Sexual-Abuse-of-Minors-by-Catholic-Priests-and-Deacons-in-the-United-States-1950-2002.pdf; and "Presbyterians Adopt Guidelines to Curb Sex Misconduct by Clergy," Associated Press, June 12, 1991: www.nytimes.com/1991/06/12/us/presbyterians-adopt-guidelines-to-curb-sex-misconduct-by-clergy.html.

[60] Pope John Paul II, Apostolic Letter *Ordinatio Sacerdotalis* (May 22, 1994), 4.

[61] St. John Vianney, *Catechism on the Priesthood*, quoted in Constance T. Hull, "Why St. John Vianney Remains a Model for the Priesthood," Catholic Exchange, Aug. 4, 2021: https://catholicexchange.com/why-st-john-vianney-remains-a-model-for-the-priesthood.

[62] See Christopher Sparks, *How Can You Still Be Catholic? 50 Answers to a Good Question* (Stockbridge, MA: Marian Press, 2017), p. 37.

[63] See Centers for Disease Control, "Child Abuse and Neglect Prevention: www.cdc.gov/child-abuse-neglect/about/about-child-sexual-abuse.html; "Facts About Child Abuse": www.childprotect.org/facts-about-child-abuse.html; "Thousands of Child Sex Abuse Cases Missed, Report Says," BBC, Nov. 24, 2015, www.bbc.com/news/uk-34904705.

[64] St. Peter Damian, *The Book of Gomorrah*, preface.

[65] Pope Francis, Letter to the People of God, Aug. 20, 2018.

[66] Quoted in Fr. Roger J. Landry, "Putting into the Deep," *The Anchor*, Aug. 14, 2009: https://catholicpreaching.com/wp/the-price-of-the-conversion-of-ars-the-anchor-august-14-2009.

[67] St. Augustine, *On the Trinity*, book XV, ch. 17: www.logoslibrary.org/augustine/trinity/1517.html.

[68] Please note that, in the case of a married couple not blessed with children, they should manifest the Holy Spirit in good works, either by adopting or fostering children, volunteering in their parish and community, or in other ways allowing the love of their marriage to overflow the bounds of the relationship between spouses into the lives and hearts of their neighbors. Our living love will adopt others into our families, whether they are blood relatives or not.

[69] St. Francis de Sales, *Introduction to the Devout Life*, part 3, ch. 38.

[70] Alice von Hildebrand, quoted in "The Meaning of Marriage," Catholic News Agency: www.catholicnewsagency.com/resource/55404/the-meaning-of-catholic-marriage.

[71] NABRE.

[72] Pope John Paul II, apostolic exhortation *Familiaris Consortio*, Nov. 22, 1981, 25.

[73] Pope Pius XI, encyclical *Casti Connubii*, Dec. 31, 1930, 27-28.

[74] See Philip Kosloski, "Fatima visionary said final battle would be over marriage and family," Aleteia, May 13, 2022: https://aleteia.org/2022/05/13/fatima-visionary-said-final-battle-would-be-over-marriage-and-family.

[75] NABRE.

[76] Ibid.

[77] For more information, see the Code of Canon Law, 1073-1107.

[78] See Jeff Ziegler, "Annulment Nation," Catholic World Report, March 2011: www.catholicculture.org/culture/library/view.cfm?recnum=9607; and Rev. W. Becket Soule, OP, "Preserving the Sanctity of Marriage: The Catholic Teaching on Annulment," Knights of Columbus, 2009: www.kofc.org/un/en/resources/cis/cis301.pdf.

[79] Fourth Lateran Council, Constitution 1: "Confession of Faith," 1215.

[80] Pope Pius IX, encyclical *Quanto Conficiamur Moerore*, Aug. 10, 1863, 7-8.

[81] Jimmy Akin, "Baptism of Desire," Catholic Answers: www.catholic.com/magazine/print-edition/baptism-of-desire.

[82] Jimmy Akin, "The *Catechism of the Catholic Church* on Islam," Catholic Answers, July 1, 2002: www.catholic.com/magazine/print-edition/the-catechism-on-islam.

[83] Pope Pius XII, encyclical *Mystici Corporis Christi*, June 29, 1943, 103.

Spiritual Reading from Fr. Chris Alar, MIC

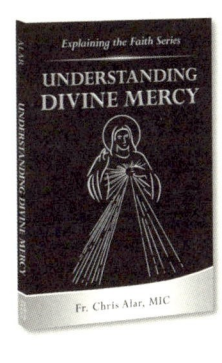

Explaining the Faith Series
Understanding Divine Mercy

The entire Divine Mercy message and devotion is summarized in one, easy-to-read book! Explaining the teaching of Jesus Christ as given to St. Faustina, *Understanding Divine Mercy* by Fr. Chris Alar, MIC, has it all. Written in his highly conversational and energetic style, this first book in his *Explaining the Faith* series will deepen your love for God and help you understand why Jesus called Divine Mercy "mankind's last hope of salvation." Paperback. 184 pages. Y128-EFBK

Explaining the Faith — DVD

Jesus' promise of Divine Mercy Sunday. Catholic devotion to Mary. Church teaching about suffering and suicide. Are you able to defend our faith when questioned about these topics and others? In this new DVD series, Fr. Chris Alar, MIC, offers his favorite 13 talks to address all of these topics and explains the Mass in a way you have never heard before. Running time: 10 hours. Y128-EXDVD

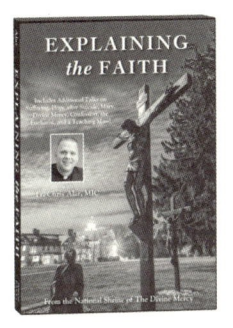

For our complete line of books, prayer cards, pamphlets, Rosaries, and chaplets, visit ShopMercy.org or call 1-800-462-7426 to have our latest catalog sent to you.

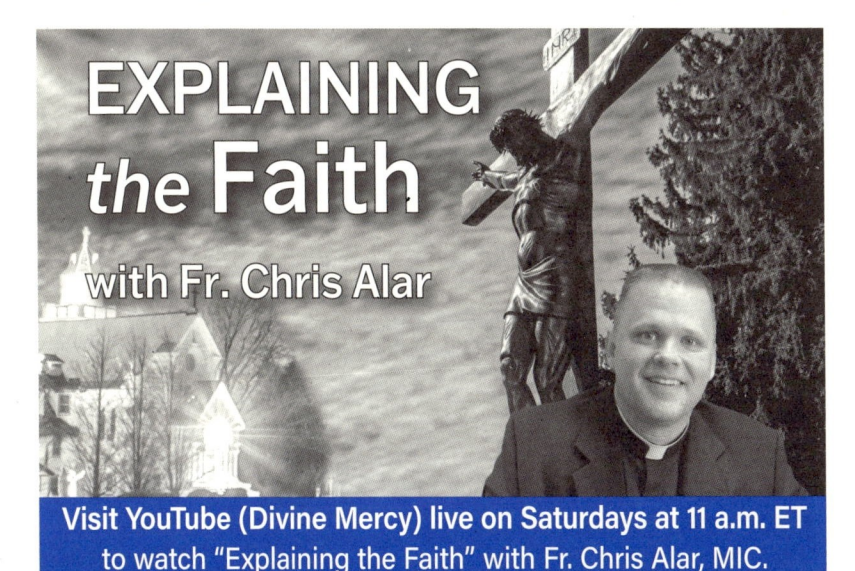

EXPLAINING *the* Faith
with Fr. Chris Alar

Visit YouTube (Divine Mercy) live on Saturdays at 11 a.m. ET to watch "Explaining the Faith" with Fr. Chris Alar, MIC. Posted afterwards on TheDivineMercy.org and DivineMercyPlus.org

Spiritual Reading from Fr. Chris Alar, MIC

After Suicide:
There's Hope For Them And For You

In this Catholic best-seller, Fr. Chris Alar, MIC, and Fr. Jason Lewis, MIC, address the hard issue of suicide simply and pastorally. Drawing from the teaching of the Church, the message of Divine Mercy, and their own experience of losing a loved one, they offer readers two key forms of hope: hope for the salvation of those who've died by their own hand, and hope for the healing of those left behind. The spiritual principles of healing and redemption apply not only to a loss from suicide, but by any means of death. Paperback. 195 pages.

Y128-ASTH

Memorialize Your Lost Loved One Online at
SuicideAndHope.com
Join other bereaved in praying for each other and for those who have taken their own lives.

Divine Mercy After Suicide: There's Still Hope
Pamphlet

Every one of us has known someone who took his or her own life, or someone whose life was affected by the suicide of a loved one. Many give up hope for those who have committed suicide and believe their souls are lost. This pamphlet explains why you should never give up on them — and what you should do instead.

Y128-HOPE

Prayer Card
A prayer for those lost to suicide from the Order of Christian Funerals.
Y128-FRJPC

The Message & Devotion of Divine Mercy

Enclosed are two helpful aids that provide the most clear and concise explanations of the Divine Mercy message and the Divine Mercy devotion. Set contains *The Message of Divine Mercy* and *The Devotion to the Divine Mercy* pamphlets. Y128-PSD

For our complete line of books, prayer cards, pamphlets, Rosaries, and chaplets, visit ShopMercy.org or call 1-800-462-7426 to have our latest catalog sent to you.

Diary of Saint Maria Faustina Kowalska: Divine Mercy in My Soul

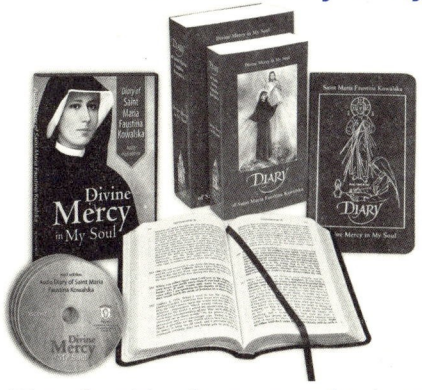

Large Paperback: Y128-NBFD
Compact Paperback: Y128-DNBF
Deluxe Leather-Bound Edition: Y128-DDBURG
Audio *Diary* MP3 Edition: Y128-ADMP3

Also available as an ebook — Visit ShopMercy.org

The *Diary* chronicles the message that Jesus, the Divine Mercy, gave to the world through this humble nun. In it, we are reminded to trust in His forgiveness — and as Christ is merciful, so, too, are we instructed to be merciful to others. Written in the 1930s, the *Diary* exemplifies God's love toward mankind and, to this day, remains a source of hope and renewal.

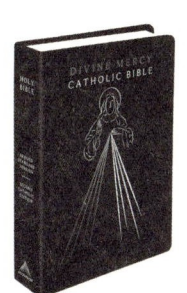

Divine Mercy Catholic Bible

Many Catholics ask what version of the Bible is best to read. In the Revised Standard Version Catholic Edition (RSV-CE) you have the answer.

As Catholics we may not realize how the revelation of Divine Mercy is interwoven into the Bible. Throughout the Bible, moments of mercy shed light on Sacred Scripture's message of God's infinite love for us.

The Divine Mercy Catholic Bible clearly shows the astounding revelation of Divine Mercy amidst the timeless truths of Sacred Scripture. This Bible includes 175 Mercy Moments and 19 articles that explain how God encounters us with mercy through His Word and Sacraments. Y128-BIDM

WATCH *Living Divine Mercy* with FR. CHRIS ALAR, MIC

THURSDAYS at 10 p.m. ET on EWTN

Posted later on TheDivineMercy.org and YouTube (Divine Mercy)

Join the
Association of Marian Helpers,
headquartered at the National Shrine of The Divine Mercy, and share in special blessings!

An invitation from
Fr. Joseph, MIC, director

Marian Helpers is an Association of Christian faithful of the Congregation of Marian Fathers of the Immaculate Conception.
By becoming a member, you share in the spiritual benefits of the daily Masses, prayers, and good works of the Marian priests and brothers.

This is a special offer of grace given to you by the Church through the Marian Fathers. Please consider this opportunity to share in these blessings, along with others whom you would wish to join into this spiritual communion.

1-800-462-7426 · Marian.org/join

The Marian Fathers of Today and Tomorrow

What are you looking for in the priests of tomorrow?

- ☑ Zeal for proclaiming the Gospel
- ☑ Faithfulness to the Pope and Church teaching
- ☑ Love of Mary Immaculate
- ☑ Love of the Holy Eucharist
- ☑ Concern for the souls in Purgatory
- ☑ Dedication to bringing God's mercy to all souls

These are the top reasons why men pursuing a priestly vocation are attracted to the Congregation of Marian Fathers of the Immaculate Conception.

Please support the education of these future priests.
More than 30 Marian seminarians are counting on your gift.

1-800-462-7426 · Marian.org/helpseminarians